POETRY (

GREAT MINDS

Your World...Your Future...YOUR WORDS

- Inspirations From The South Of England
Edited by Bobby Tobolik

 Young**Writers**

First published in Great Britain in 2005 by:
Young Writers
Remus House
Coltsfoot Drive
Peterborough
PE2 9JX
Telephone: 01733 890066
Website: www.youngwriters.co.uk

SB ISBN 1 84602 286 X

Foreword

This year, the Young Writers' 'Great Minds' competition proudly presents a showcase of the best poetic talent selected from over 40,000 up-and-coming writers nationwide.

Young Writers was established in 1991 to promote the reading and writing of poetry within schools and to the youth of today. Our books nurture and inspire confidence in the ability of young writers and provide a snapshot of poems written in schools and at home by budding poets of the future.

The thought, effort, imagination and hard work put into each poem impressed us all and the task of selecting poems was a difficult but nevertheless enjoyable experience.

We hope you are as pleased as we are with the final selection and that you and your family continue to be entertained with *Great Minds - Inspirations From The South Of England* for many years to come.

Contents

Megi Dumani (12) 59
Carl Baird (12) 59
Dumi Nkomo (13) 60
Adrian Shaw (12) 61
Hollie Morris (12) 61
Samantha Dix (14) 62
Holly Hereford (14) 63
Anni Tucker (12) 64
Kayleigh Gillane (12) 64
Rosa Liotti (12) 65
Charlotte Edwards (12) 65
Lauren Baker (12) 66
Waqas Butt (12) 66
Amy Alderton (12) 67
Nathan Neal (12) 67
Luke O'Keefe (12) 68
Billie Smout (12) 68
Ricky Taylor (12) 69
Shannon Markland (13) 69
Jon Christey (12) 70

Kingsmead School, Enfield
Joanna Lyons (15) 70
Cera Alp (15) 71
Danielle Yeates (15) 72
Hazel Marzetti (15) 73

Oxted School, Oxted
Jamie Parish (12) 74
Chris Heyburn (13) 74
Lucy Gorringe (14) 75

St Birinus School, Didcot
Josh Elford (13) 75
Sam Reynolds (13) 76
Richard Tyler (12) 76
Nathan Reeve (13) 77
Ollie Ealey (14) 77
Daniel Griffiths 78
Matthew Swan (13) 78
Tom Tatford (12) 78

Aaron Jane (13)   79
Nick Ingrem (13)   79
Lewis Brown (13)   79
Cameron Stanton (13)   80
Anthony Lyford (13)   80
Luke Jepson (13)   81

St John The Baptist Catholic School, Woking

Joseph Kent   81
Lauren Bradfield   82
Siobhan Cawkwell   83
Louise McGovern   84
Jessica Loveridge   85
Joe Holt   86
Christina Derisi   87
Emily Buzaglo   88
Bronwyn White   89
Zoe Etter (12)   89
Bernadette Cross   90
Georgia Vardy   90
Elliott Burrowes (13)   91

St Martin's School, Northwood

James Taylor (11)   91
Breman Rajkumar (13)   92
Nikhil Patel (13)   92
Vidit Doshi (11)   93
David Cussons (10)   93
Richard Gallagher (13)   94
James Elliott-Vincent (13)   94
Sanjiv Pandya (11)   95
Vincent Moses (13)   95

St Paul's Way Community School, Tower Hamlets

Noorjahan Chowdhury (14)   96
Shaun Newman (13)   97
Hameema Khanom (12)   98

St Philomena's RC High School for Girls, Carshalton

Reisha McKay (13)   98

Eleanor Wise (13)	99
Daniela Fichera (13)	99
Kirsten Sullivan (12)	100
Madi Barwick (13)	100
Amber Chandler (13)	101
Sarah Hallam (13)	101
Mariah Wilde (13)	102
Alysia Haughton-Nicholls (13)	102
Philomena Da Silva (13)	103
Francesca Hayward (13)	103
Faune Hyland (13)	104
Sorcha O'Byrne (13)	104
Charlotte Dulake (13)	105
Ania Giemza (13)	105
Alexandra Bradford (13)	106
Lauren O'Sullivan (13)	106
Emily Page (13)	107
Sarah Audisho (13)	107
Amy Sharp (12)	108
Aimee Allen (13)	108
Nicola Kyei (13)	109
Emma Lucas (13)	109
Madeleine Cloonan (13)	110
Stephanie Long (13)	111
Annabelle Downey (13)	112
Kate Landowska (13)	113
Harriet Goonetillake (12)	113
Anna Desborough (13)	114
Amanda Watling (12)	114
Ellen Wilson (13)	115
Charlotte Holmes (13)	115
Siân Darcy (13)	116
Amilia Csepreghi (13)	117
Claire Raftery (13)	117
Cassandra Simpson (13)	118
Arianna Tinnirello (13)	119
Megan Ball (13)	120

Sarah Bonnell School, Stratford

Rene Frimpong-Manso (14)	120
Fazaila Hussnain Bukhari (14)	121

The Sholing Technology College, Southampton

Tolworth Girls' School, Surbiton

Judith Zendle (14)	187
Karen Wood (14)	187
Jade Phillips (14)	188
Fagae Asghari (14)	188
Hannah Kerly (14)	189
Alice Green (14)	189
Katie Launder Glass (14)	190
Robyn Ward (14)	191
Alka Patel (14)	192
Gurpreet Kalsi (14)	192

Tormead School, Guildford

Sophie Finney (15)	193
Emily Adams-Cairns (15)	194
Claire Hallybone (15)	195

Trevelyan Middle School, Windsor

Paige Harper (10)	195
Kirstie Harman (11)	196
Jack Harrold (10)	196
James Napier (10)	196
Tessa Kirby (10)	197
Thomas Moran (10)	197
Angela Cracknell (10)	198
Bryce Kane (11)	198
Lottie Mudge (10)	198
Tom Flower (10)	199
Robert Moran (11)	199
George Peryer (11)	199
Andrew Holmes (10)	200
Grant White (10)	200
Mellissa Watson (11)	201
Emily Gifford (10)	201
Blair McHarg (10)	202
Gabby Killick (11)	202
Hannah Ward (11)	202
Grace Bradbury (10)	203
Amy Balchin (10)	203
Sophie Ellis (11)	203
Ria Chaudry (10)	204
Rosie Wege (10)	204

The Poems

Escape

My secret's getting hard to keep,
The more I think, the more I need to speak.
My father's yelling down the phone,
When's my mum gonna come back home?
My brother, him, well he's gone out,
I close my mouth before I shout.
I need to run far away,
'Cause if I stay, it'll all come out.
My father's gone, it's now my chance,
But I stop and think of Mum.
I convince myself that she'll be fine.
I shut the door, I leave no note,
I run,
Run on,
I'm free at last.

Nadia Richards (13)
Alperton Community School, Wembley

Alone

Here I stand without any light,
I, without any love,
Alone I stand.

No one wants me,
No one likes me,
No one needs me.
Since there's no love,
My heart has gone cold.
Since there's no love,
My heart has gone hard.
That makes me so mad,
I miss what I had.
It makes me all sad.

Diviya Uthayakumar (12)
Alperton Community School, Wembley

My Dream

As we were walking hand in hand
Along the gold and shiny sand

I was feeling great like I was on cloud nine
I have now crossed that thin blue line

The one that leads between me and him
I feel so good, I wish I could swim

Far out into the sea to God my Father
I am so happy, I laugh harder and harder

The sun is high in the bright blue sky
And little birds are flying by

The sea is blue and very calm
I scooped up some sand into my palm

I want to fall asleep on this beach forever
For this sand is as soft as a feather

When morning comes and I lie still on the sand
All I'll need is a musical band

To complete this feeling I have inside
If only I could take a ride

With my love to get married
And my dress so long it has to be carried

Goodnight
Goodnight
Goodnight.

Isis Watson (13)
Alperton Community School, Wembley

My Class

In our class
Boys and girls work together
Throughout the day
Whatever the weather
Left and right
Boys and girls in sight
Always giving a helping hand
Working together as a band
My class is a happy team
Always happy, never mean.

Emmanuel Adjerese (13)
Alperton Community School, Wembley

Hatred

Hate is like the sun,
Burning gently in space.
Every day getting hotter and hotter,
Closer and closer to Earth.

Until one day it strikes hard.

On that day the world starts to cook,
Simmering under the sun's wrath,
Burning under hate's power,
Closer and closer to death.

Love is gone forever.

Hate doesn't give second chances,
The sun can't stop for love,
Love can be strong,
But hate can be stronger.

Life is tough, but don't hate it,
Because it will hate you back.

Alice Young (12)
Battle Abbey School, Battle Abbey

Open Windows

This window has no bars or panes of glass,
But it helps you view opportunities,
And it helps those who are stuck to see what,
When they are all older, they will become.
Will they be rich, poor, happy or neither?
Will they become a good provider?
But as usual in reality,
Will we know? Will it be a mystery?

So many times I've tried to discover,
Whether I will be stupid or clever.
That constant feeling of wonder,
Drove me crazy, I began to ponder.
I started to sit and write this poem,
About what I'll be and where I'm going.

Elliot Foster (14)
Battle Abbey School, Battle Abbey

Changing Feelings

Oh, how I'm feeling so drizzly this day,
As flowers and grasses are hurt from winds.
My mind is dulled, this supposed gay May,
As the winds and rains whistle their weird ways.
But soon I hope this day will be passing,
And future days will beam with sunshine, gleaming.
My bones are fed, lifting light, love, laughter.
From rays of warmth, comfort, but time seeming
To leave, senseless and stepping sleeplessly
Into the mist of a shadowed place.
Shivers are sent like knives effortlessly
Easing through the silent, static, still space.
My mind hopes and prays for a light to arise
As ghosts do rise, for dreams I do despise.

Tim Plail (14)
Battle Abbey School, Battle Abbey

Mirrors Sonnet

You stand there seeing your own reflection,
If your second self tells you what to do,
Why is all you see lies and deception?
This is the one person you can't see through,
Sometimes you can see your own face distort.
You may just wonder if that person pale,
Is you, just for the sake of mindless thought.
Your iife is one big ocean, sail or fail,
Reflections can stare at you, hard, long,
Is that you in those glassy and frail shards?
Look away, turn around, glance back, it's gone,
Is life one of God's many playing cards?
Know you must be the person you accept,
Look back on yourself, make sure you reflect.

Willow Rolfe (14)
Battle Abbey School, Battle Abbey

Mirrors

What can I do? I can show truth or lies,
But I will never let you see inside.
Gaze into the eyes of the reflection,
Distorting yourself in my deception.
Your eyes will see what they want you to see,
But your reflection shows the truth in me.
Your shape can look the same through your own eyes,
But through mine I can create and tell lies.
Sometimes I can be a little two-faced,
So be warned and come within your own pace.
Stare into my depths and look at what's there,
Take your time and study your face with care.
So this is everything that I can do,
Turn yourself around and I will show you.

Sarah Bridger (14)
Battle Abbey School, Battle Abbey

Forget-Me-Not

Don't forget me
When I'd lie awake on 'miss you nights'
And wait for you to return to our love.
Don't forget me
When we would dance to the night's song and wait,
Wait for day to come. But the view is bleak,
And the night's simple song is out of tune.
The only hand I'd stroke is in my mem'ry.
But although I have nothing left,
I still own your sweet touch that shall never,
That shall never, leave my innocent soul. I remember
The wild summer; and the magical spring.
I remember the cold winter's night that
Whistled and screamed, but you made the loud screams
Choruses. The forget-me-not, so near
To perfect; yet so far from me.

Claire Petzal (14)
Battle Abbey School, Battle Abbey

Youth

When we were young, age was just a concept,
We never knew that life would move this fast.
We would dream of being older except,
When we do, we wish to relive the past.
Old age seemed a million years away,
For us, growing up seemed for us to choose.
But the laws of time we have to obey,
I wish that I'd known then, the time I'd lose.
I would have stopped and taken some more time,
To appreciate the world as it was.
When I was naive, the world was sublime,
But in my old age I realised I was lost.
As time goes by, the older you become,
Understand, youth is wasted on the young.

Rosie Wakeham (13)
Battle Abbey School, Battle Abbey

Lonely

(This poem is about a homeless child)

Life is so lonely.
So cold.
So bare.
People walk past without a care.

I shiver in the rags I've been wearing for months.
No warmth.
No love.
People push and shove.

I wonder why.
Haven't they felt lonely before?
Why don't they care?
Haven't they got just a penny to spare?

I'm only twelve.
It's not my fault.
Why don't you wonder why I'm here?
I spend every day in worry and fear.

Life is so lonely.
So cold.
So bare.
People walk past without a care.

Hannah Bretton (14)
Battle Abbey School, Battle Abbey

Battle

On the battlefield murder goes on,
Death . . . death . . . death . . .
Soldiers shielding everywhere
From the arrows flying through the air,
Falling, falling, soldiers murdered.
They're dead, the battle's over;
Win, lose, it doesn't matter.
It shouldn't have started and it's all my fault.

Lukas Choppen (13)
Battle Abbey School, Battle Abbey

Banish The Dawn

Here, deep in my darkness, a rising dawn,
I flee from the night and its moonlit scorn.

I crave for the patience to sit and wait,
Though it's a thing I have done too much of late,
A fear of the dark, and a stilted cry,
These foreign creatures in their native sky.

In this foreign land, in this foreign field,
I feel burning in scars not yet fully healed,
The pain in my mind, not one soon to ease,
Yearning for home and a soft summer breeze.

And so the sun shall rise a year too late,
One more day to kill those I do not hate,
I beg to spare me grief and spare me pain,
For I know I cannot face the dawn again.

Sophie Petzal (14)
Battle Abbey School, Battle Abbey

Living A Life Of Abuse

She beats me repeatedly every night
With her fist in my face she hits me hard
She says it's only fair as I'm not bright.
I cried inside and thus now I am scarred
It's not only the physical abuse, but mentally too.
With the names, remarks,
Embarrassment, that's all she has to use.
It's my innocent words that start the sparks.
She said she never wanted me to come
It was a mistake from the beginning
This world is only big enough for one.
She threatens me my life will be ending
But I carry on living a life of abuse
For this is how I feel some sort of use.

Emilie Moffat (14)
Battle Abbey School, Battle Abbey

Unexpected And Unprepared

People would say I am outgoing and a bubbly person
And I suppose so would I
I live my life to the fullest and am not scared to take a risk,
But I have loads more things I want to do, and will do,
Until I can settle down with my husband.
You're only young once.

Rock climbing, abseiling, snowboarding
And a million other things too!
Scuba-diving, paragliding, bungee-jumping
I really have lots more to do.

But then one day in the shower
This thing I feel has incredible power
This lump I did not expect
Changes my life into a whirlpool of emotions
And with respect
I was not ready to die.

The treatment's bad
I've lost all my hair
Because of this lump, I feel so mad
And all this stress just builds up inside
I am not going to live by my partner's side.

Because 'until death us do part' is what they say
But not like this, not today
I'm getting weaker, I can hardly breathe
All my goals I can no more achieve.

This is not the way I wanted to go
I'm still young, 27, please God no
But as it gets worse
I accept that this time you have defeated me.
So goodbye.

Natasha Bristowe (14)
Battle Abbey School, Battle Abbey

The Anger Of A Troubled Soul

I can feel something boil and swell inside me,
Something that I just cannot stop,
No matter how hard I try.
It's something that has nagged away at me for a long time gone,
Something that ever grows until it dies,
No matter how much it falsely cools.
At first, a mere hollow hawk gaining on a vole,
Then the lion strikes on the heedless prey,
The damage extracted, never undone,
It erupts like a raging volcano, asleep at first, then alive again,
Ne'er to be extinct for long enough,
No matter how close it comes,
But at last, alas, the hard waves lapse,
The storm subsides and the conflict ends,
The bitter winds draw back and the horizon clears,
With the siege of sense overcome,
But all active energy is lost,
But those loyal few who remain behind,
Help that lost soul on to the road to forgiveness.

Henry Huggett (13)
Battle Abbey School, Battle Abbey

Arsenal

Red on the green
That's my team!
The mighty Gunners
Shooting down the opposition
Fans waving and screaming
Whenever they're on a winning streak
They always win
They never lose
But if they do
They're still the best.

Claire Hunt (14)
Bognor Regis Community College, Bognor Regis

Flower Power

There's a flower in the field,
All alone and unhappy,
The leaves dried up and crisp,
Not a spot of green on the broken brown leaves,
The stem lifeless with no energy,
Petals no more,
Two left,
Colourless,
Given up hope to impress,
So small, motionless and inert.

But just think, not so long ago,
I used to impress,
Many came from miles away to see the vibrant colours,
The leaves waiting to catch the chilled rain.

But no more,
Now just a sad,
Pathetic,
Loner,
Me.
The flower is me.

Kylie Skilton (14)
Bognor Regis Community College, Bognor Regis

The Old Woods

The cheeps and the chirps of the wild birds
The grunts and groans of the giant creatures
The crack and crunch of the sticks and twigs
The crinkling and rustling of the old oak trees
The hollering and howling of the winter wind
The pitter-patter of the falling rain
These are the sounds of an old worn out wood.

Sam Chant (13)
Bognor Regis Community College, Bognor Regis

Life Cycle

A flower is a human being,
The all-knowing,
All-seeing.
Every year it lives,
Its knowledge grows,
Until gradually,
The growing *slows.*
The petals start to flutter
To the ground,
As the years of your life
T
  u
    m
      b
        l
          e
Down.
The leaves start to wither,
Your skin starts to sag,
Proceeding to droop,
But in a way glad,
For after death comes life,
As the flower uncurls,
A baby is born,
Introduced to the world.

Bethany Higgs (14)
Bognor Regis Community College, Bognor Regis

No Mercy

(Based on 'Stealing' by Carol-Anne Duffy)

How did I turn out like this?
I have no idea.
Sometimes I get really down,
Then I puff on a fag
And I'm calm again.

I'd rather be here than some poxy kids' home.
Loneliness. Nobody understands what it's like.
Then I see a mate stood on the corner,
I breathe a sigh of relief - *aah*.

Sometimes I nick things to stay sane,
Keys left carelessly under plant pots,
No one knows about me,
An undetectable thief - no mess left.

When I'm annoyed,
The elderly and nursery kids
Flinch when they see me.
My eyes dancing like balls of fire,
Inhaling their terror,
I smile maliciously.

Sadness. Friends who aren't true
Like mine. But who else have I got?
For it's a dog eat dog world,
Show no mercy.

Shria Suchak (13)
Brighton and Hove High School, Brighton

Murder

(Based on 'Stealing' by Carol-Anne Duffy)

The last time I broke the law? Last week.
Murder. Walking down the street; a tall, black man
Under the night sky. Sudden anger
Rushed through me. I wanted to hurt him.

I crept slowly towards him, my pale hands
Stretched out. They looked almost ghostly,
Glowing in the dark night. I slipped one
Into my pocket, and drew out a silver knife.

The man froze. Perhaps he could sense me
Glaring at his back. His head turned, as I
Ducked under a bench on the path. He shrugged
And continued walking. I sighed,
A sigh of relief - *aah.*

I crawled out from under the bench,
And gripped the knife. Taking a deep breath,
I grabbed the black man's collar
And stabbed him. He didn't deserve to live.

He let out a scream, which filled
Me with joy. As he collapsed, I
Escaped into the dark. Left his body
Lying there. Even when I explain why I did it,
People never understand. You don't either, do you?

Jennifer Shaw (12)
Brighton and Hove High School, Brighton

A River

A river stream is a racetrack
That bites into the earth
It gallops and gallops all down the track
But at the last hurdle . . .

Down and down it falls
With its horse hooves grasping for the ground
The tail of the beast splashes in the mud
It gallops and gallops until . . .

Splash!
The hooves hit the ground
The saddle waves in the air
But the stirring stops
All is still, all is silent

But nothing is still forever
And the fidgety beast trots away
Down and down around and around
Like a whirlpool

It twists and turns
Without control
Falling and tripping
And with its final cry
It stops . . . and washes up on the shore.

Michael Garvey (13)
Charters School, Ascot

Dragonfly

The patchwork quilt stretched out below me,
Everything is as silent as a fish.
The squirrels' manors are great trees,
The land and country stretched out before me on a silver plate.

My long and leathery wings,
Like the hide of a rhino,
Buzz at light speed.
My size a useful weapon,
My antennae taste the air around.

I'm watching,
I'm waiting,
I'm hovering.

And then I see it waiting for me,
I dive, darting through the air at light speed.
I slow and float, regain my sense of direction.

It takes me halfway down,
Through the clear glass of the air
I smash.

My prey,
It waits.

Again I dive, thrashing my wings wildly,
But I spin out of control,
A lucky escape some might say.

Tom Buckley (11)
Charters School, Ascot

Firefly

I hover in the air,
In the moonlit sky.
I am at romantic places,
To make humans feel happier.
You have to wrap up warm
To find me.
The temperature's quite cold,
It is also very damp where I live
And the thunderstorms are wild.

I'm rather small in size,
So I'm rather hard to see,
But when the sun goes down,
I shine very brightly.
My wings are very delicate, as delicate as lace,
Not forgetting my thin, stick-like legs
That tuck underneath my small, raisin-like body.
I don't need good eyesight, but a great sense of smell.
Finally, I have a small mouth to gobble up young, squishy insects.

I sit there waiting on a leaf,
For a juicy greenfly to float by.
Then I see it . . . I dart at it
And suck until it's in my mouth.
I chew rapidly and swallow
And go in search of another tasty meal.

I soar in the dark, starry sky
And land on a lily pad in the pond.
Then I see . . . a toad.
I fly high, I will find a new place to settle.

Olivia Kemp (12)
Charters School, Ascot

Slugs

My name's Slug, James Slug.

You find me mostly on the floor,
On some shelves, or on a door.
I very slowly squelch along,
Singing quietly my famous song,
Do-d-do-dum,
Rum-pum-pum.

I carefully but slowly slide around,
Clinging and sticking to the ground.
My body looks slimy, but feels sticky,
Makes my missions rather tricky.
I feel quite bumpy,
Which makes me look frumpy.

I'm looking around to find a shell,
To swap to be a snail, to do my mission well.
I drag my tail slowly behind,
It leaves a trail for others to find.

I'll find a shell someday soon,
Under sun or under moon.
A shell I see!
It's just waiting for me.

Emily Elliott (12)
Charters School, Ascot

Caterpillar's Journey

I am down on the muddy ground
Looking for food.
I feel hot and flustered
I can hear the rustling leaves.

My rough, green skin is like a crocodile's
My eyes are small and black.
Inside I am soft like a marshmallow
My antennae are minute, you cannot see them.

I sit and eat
I rest a while.
I crawl up a gigantic tree
I scurry around in the treetops.

I see a moth and a butterfly
They have inspired me.
I wonder which I will become
I guess soon enough I will find out.

Inside my cocoon I feel so snug
I cannot wait to find out what I've become.
I unfold my wings and fly
I have transformed into a butterfly.

Fong Chin (12)
Charters School, Ascot

All About Me By Milli The Millipede

Hi, my name's Milli the millipede,
I travel at an amazing speed,
I have a lovely house made of weeds,
Which is in a garden right next to the sea.

My family, now where do I begin?
My mum works full time in a tin
Which says Heinz Baked Beans on the rim.
My brother and sister are both normal and dim.

Now more about me.
I'm as small as can be
And I scuttle on a stroll at the sea,
Where I meet up with my friend called Fred the flea.

I look like a dark stick with 100 legs,
Which look like small, plastic clothes pegs.
My eyes are as pearly as pearls in the sea,
But still I manage to vaguely see!

Adam Snowden (12)
Charters School, Ascot

The Streets Of London

People rush around like ants delivering food to the nest,
Thousands of legs moving like a centipede,
Different markets with beggars next to them,
Waiting for the owners to turn a blind eye.
Sudden applause from the people watching the street
As a man blows fire like an angry dragon,
People pushing past as if the street needs to be twice as wide,
Sometimes the cry of a chimney sweep fills the street,
Loud voices fill the air,
The street is so loud, it is nearly as loud as an airport.
Every now and then a policeman walks past,
A baton in his hand like a club to hit you,
The smell of freshly baked bread
Wafts over everyone like a cloud over the sun.

Amy Richardson (13)
Charters School, Ascot

A Day In The Life Of An Ant Worker

Do you know
I'm here underground
Probably not
Because I make no sound.

Mounds of earth
Are a clue
To a maze of tunnels
Beneath the pine needles covered in dew.

Three parts I have to my body
Two delicate feelers on my head
If you look closely, you'll see
I'm jet-black and crimson-red.

Six long legs spring from my middle
Smooth and nimble, I am fast
Carrying the queen's eggs
I can't be last.

In pursuit of food I go
Organised but in a hurry
Taking the route of the others
Follow that scent, I scurry.

A dragonfly
Oh, what a teatime treat
Struggling, we drag him home
Cheered on by other creatures we meet.

Another day is done
But a worker cannot rest
Eggs have hatched and must be fed
So much to do, but just time to tidy the nest.

Stacey Brown (12)
Charters School, Ascot

Butterfly Life

I am in a family's garden,
It is a boiling summer's day.
I smell the sweet flowers,
I am sitting on a soft bush.
My wings are like a stained glass window,
My small, round eyes look around.
I don't have a shell to make me hot,
I am a small butterfly for my age.
I am waiting for a tiny droplet of water
Because at the moment I am starting to wither.
I move like the wind,
I can fly very fast.
I just wish sometimes that I could crawl down on the ground.
My journey is taking me to my small, quiet home,
Getting away from the sun is my aim today.
I am home at last,
Now I am going to take a long nap.

Amy Funnell (12)
Charters School, Ascot

Cave

The echo of dripping water nearby,
The rocks, sitting like boulders in your way,
The crumbly walls break away the moment you touch them,
The darkness, the dampness.

The dusty, cobweb-filled tunnels and paths,
Those imaginary sounds of the space scare you,
The door is locked, there's no way out,
The darkness, the dampness.

Claire Turle (13)
Charters School, Ascot

Kitchen Menaces

Scurrying across the kitchen floor,
Fighting for food,
Tiny little crumbs lying innocently,
Waiting silently, praying,
Until little creatures come along.
The ants have approached,
Their charcoal-black bodies
As hard as rocks,
Though as soft as a sponge, when a human comes.
Antennae swishing in the chilly air,
Eyes darting for the predator,
Until the ants escape,
Out of the dark kitchen,
Into a hole, getting darker,
Darker, darker . . .
Then gone.

Rhianne Blochley (12)
Charters School, Ascot

Frozen Rain

Waves of water lash at your back,
Cold, foamy ice trickles down your neck,
Your feet sink in the squelching sand,
The salted water smashes on your head,
Your feet crush the shells.
The feeling of getting nowhere,
Sharks bite into your shoes,
Your hair blows in the sea breeze,
The waves obstruct your only view.

Emily Bolland (13)
Charters School, Ascot

Vegi Ball Game

The colourful crowds of
    Vegetation scream
As you walk down the Manchester
    Red street
Green football cabbages
    Are flying
As you join the stadium
    Crowds

Mobs of vegetables are
    Arrested
And are taken
    Away
Traitor carrots are bagged and
    Carried off
And then chopped into
    Little pieces.

James Innes (13)
Charters School, Ascot

Chimney Sweeps

Every morning rain or shine
The chimney sweep climbs up high
His brush twirls round and round
That dirty chimney full of grime.

The chimney sweep works long and hard
Black dust falls all around
His hands are covered with soot
It even covers his sad little eyes.

Philippa Colborn (13)
Charters School, Ascot

Rainbows Of Fruit And Veg

Fruit and vegetables
Lounging in baskets
Like flurries of colour
In a deep sea
Of reds and yellows
A rainbow reflecting
Onto the concrete road
A riot of colours
Screaming at me
With a mixture of
Anger and happiness
Floating in a puddle of emotions
Tins of paint
Glimmering in the afternoon
Each eager to be the first taken
And let out a
Burst of shining colour
Into the crisp, sunny air.

Charlotte Shuter (13)
Charters School, Ascot

Fruitiveg

As the oranges enter the battlefield,
The turnips and the carrots surrender,
The apples are hungry, they are holding off the spinach,
The bananas have too much to do,
They shoot the turnips, it had to be done.

The peach proves too much for the lettuce,
As the tomatoes melt down.

Richard George (12)
Charters School, Ascot

Slug

Slowly
Sliding
Lunging
Lazily
Ugly
Goo.

Sack of slime
I feel
I am
My puny eyes
Stuck on stalks
Bending and twisting
All at my own pace.

My blank face
No expression
Underneath
One row of teeth
A boring and unbalanced diet
Leaf by leaf
Despite my ugliness
I leave behind
A wonderful trail of glitter.

Michael Beck (12)
Charters School, Ascot

Flyaway Fly

Here I sit peacefully,
On the checked picnic mat,
Like a never-ending field of food,
The very thought of which,
Makes my mouth water
And my body churn with hunger.
My delicate wings twitch,
Anxious to be flying,
My eyes are like pinpricks
And my legs are string.
You could say I'm soft and furry,
But not like a teddy.
My body is black as death.
Waiting,
Watching,
I make my move,
Fluttering my wings
And darting about.
Across the picnic mat I fly,
Landing beside the cakes.
Swat!

Beki Sherrington (12)
Charters School, Ascot

Trapped In A Cellar

The cellar is dark, like a cave,
With a patch of light shining through
From some hole I cannot seem to find,
Giving fresh, wonderful air to breathe.

An eerie sound of dripping
Leaks from sticky bottles of wine,
Tiny, quick footsteps
Scurry and hurry in fear.

I smell a horrid stench of a thing I can't see,
Of something rotting in the corner.
Maybe that's what's causing this damp, warm air
Or maybe it's the radiator upstairs.

A dead rat on the floor,
Sends shivers up my spine.
I wonder if my friend is still up there,
Waiting for me to escape?

Daniel Chiu (13)
Charters School, Ascot

I Wish I Was A Butterfly

Colours, colours everywhere,
Flying high in the air,
O, I wish I could fly,
O, I wish I was a butterfly.

Red, purple, orange, blue,
All the colours of me and you,
Green, yellow, pink and black,
All these colours they'll never lack.

Rainbow colours, make them shine,
Like a stained glass window so fine,
Hear the flutter, flap, flap, flap,
Careful of them butterfly traps.

Light I like, so able to land,
I would love to be held in someone's hand,
Let me fly, high up into the sky,
O, I wish I was a butterfly.

Zoë Way (12)
Charters School, Ascot

Dragonfly

The red-hot desert so hot to touch,
So dry and covered in hairline cracks,
Cracks, like cracks in china cups.

My body so long, streamlined, so delicate
And yet so small compared to desert creatures.
My glass-like wing covered in a layer of turquoise tissue paper,
Thin, but hard to destroy.
As I hover over the barren desert,
My veiny wings flutter up and down.
My eyes are blanketed with a transparent layer of thin plastic.

I watch,
I wait,
I hover, trying to look for water.

As I fly, I buzz,
As I hover, I sting,
As I stop, silence covers the area,
No sound to be heard.

I can see an oasis ahead of me,
Water trickling and leaves tumbling,
The heavens have opened,
I have found my home,
My favourite place in the world.

Katie Gow (11)
Charters School, Ascot

Cellar

Cellar . . . cellar . . . cellar . . .
I'm stuck down here in this box.
Someone please help me.
It's dark and cold,
There's cobwebs everywhere,
Attaching to me as I pass through them.
Spiders are weaving in and out of my fingers.
I hear the lock crash to the floor.
I wonder to myself if there's someone there.
I can't see where I'm placing my feet,
As I stumble through a shadow,
A shadow of a rusty chair.
I sit myself down to rest my legs.
I hear a loud *bang!*
I run up the concrete stairs,
Clonk, clonk, the sound of my shoes.
I finally reach the top.
I see light, I see light!
The wide door creaks open.
I have been rescued from the . . .
Cellar . . . cellar . . . cellar.

Charlotte Stevenson (13)
Charters School, Ascot

The Market

There are bells ringing and people singing,
Little pesky kids sticking their fingers in lovely handmade cakes.
There are dogs hovering around meat stalls
And I can hear the market people's calls.
By the end of the day the street is all bare
And no more noise, just quiet.

Laura Potbury (13)
Charters School, Ascot

The Philosophy

What is this air we breathe?
Is this the nectar of life?
As I dream, I see children playing,
Like ambassadors of joy,
I imagine birds soaring on a summer's dawn,
Freely showing the gift of life.

But I must leave and be struck by reality,
For the wonderland's destiny is to perish in my mind,
The light is extinguished by the prowess of black.

Now, I am back to this familiar, yet alien world,
Plagued by inhumane conflicts running rife,
Destroyed by the domination of greed.
Condemned to a lifetime of eternal war.
The heart of man being overthrown
By the anger and hatred and deceit.
The rhythm of life has been altered in such an irreparable way.

As I say this, it was God who made the dark and the light,
The good and the evil,
And it is God who knows
The light will always conquer the dark,
For someone somewhere, will always keep the light shining.

Nikhil Thakral (11)
Claremont School, St Leonards-on-Sea

The Indian Princess

All alone she sits on a summer's day,
Sitting alone underneath the old tree,
Lost because she has forgotten the way
To show her love to the man at sea.

He has forgotten her young, smiling face,
As he sits in the stern he remembers,
His time at her beautiful palace,
And the glow of the old fire's embers.

But then he left the beautiful princess,
For the maharajah said to cease,
'My child's face is not for you to caress,
Say it is over and leave her in peace.'

So the young sailor did as he was told,
And now they remember those days of old.

Jessica Scotton (13)
Dunottar School, Reigate

Don't Know What To Write!

Now I've put pen to paper
I don't know what to write
I could write about something scary
That will give the judges a fright.
What about something hairy?
But that will be a bit strange
There is a range to what I can write
How about a kite?
Yeah, that will be alright.
I'm like an explorer lost in a desert
Trying to find help.

Joe Hearn (13)
Finchley Catholic High School, Finchley

Make Poverty History

Make poverty history
Right now
People are dying
Right now

It was on the telly
All day long
We helped them a bit
By singing songs

We're OK
On the phone
The others just
Walk alone

Are you sure
You've done all you can?
Have you helped yourself
Or have you helped them?

Jack Cronin (13)
Finchley Catholic High School, Finchley

Heaven

Words can't explain it,
For you have not been there before.
It's blue with golden gates,
Leading to the great big door.
Beyond is unbelievable,
With a floor of great, strong clouds.
With things unimaginable,
It's quiet, not loud.
It's a good place to go,
If you're good,
So be a great person
And you will go there,
You really should.

Raphael Narnor (13)
Finchley Catholic High School, Finchley

The Sea

Golden sand,
It runs through your hands.
Beneath the shore,
There is a shining door,
That leads to more.

It is a peaceful place,
Where we can face,
The ocean.
People are here for their holidays,
So they can relax and enjoy sunny days,
In the sun.

They get a suntan,
And go as red as a frying pan,
They have lots of fun,
In the sun.

Alex Greene (13)
Finchley Catholic High School, Finchley

Kris

I have a friend called Kris
When I walked past him, he would hiss
He's as weird as weird can be
So one day I decided to invite him to tea

He has two incredibly big teeth
With which he ate all the beef
He's got a massive head
And everyone wishes he was dead

My poem has come to an end
He was a guy who truly drove me round the bend.

Martin Edmett (13)
Finchley Catholic High School, Finchley

School

School is good, school is bad,
We say they're the best times you've had.
You have so many subjects,
You don't learn a lot,
Teachers say to pupils,
'Have you lost the plot?'

We have so many holidays,
So we can take a break,
When we are ill,
They say it was a fake.

When we finish school,
We stand behind our desks and pray,
Then we go home and rest,
Until another school day.

David Flynn (13)
Finchley Catholic High School, Finchley

I Want To Be A Rock Star, Star, Star

I love music, it is my life,
When I strummed my first guitar,
The blood rushed faster through my body.
The sound was amazing, so loud and strong
And then that second I knew what I wanted to be,
A rock star, star, star.
I met up with my friends that day
And told them my ideas,
We started a band.
I was that much closer to being
A rock star, star, star.
I am now older and my life is great because
I am a rock star, star, star.

Marco Sidoli (13)
Finchley Catholic High School, Finchley

War

I was the one who pulled the trigger of that gun,
I ended the lives of people as I saw them run,
If only,
If only,
I could control my actions,
It made me feel sad to see people's reactions,
Fighting for my country,
Defending my religion,
Planting bombs in different regions,
Which destroy a number of big buildings and places,
I am destruction, not to be part of the human race,
I am a big disgrace.
People losing loved ones as their heartbeat starts to race,
I am the one that makes people sad and depressed,
I am War.
Stop it!

Philip Bosah (13)
Finchley Catholic High School, Finchley

Rugby

Rugby, a great game to play,
A game full of violence, aggression and pain.

Rugby, what a great way,
To get rid of anger, frustration and shame.

Rugby, a game with a scrum,
Run into the wrong person, you'll end up flat on your bum.

Rugby, a game with a kick,
Real hard runs and real hard hits.

Rugby, a great game to play,
Even though I'm short, it's still my favourite sport.

Tom McGoey (13)
Finchley Catholic High School, Finchley

Children

Children are children, who like to play,
They are very messy when they're dealing with clay.
Kids like to go to the park and have lots of fun,
While their parents are getting a tan under the sun.
They scream, shout and play about,
Girls in Brownies and boys in Scouts.
I wish I could go back and be a child,
Those days were wicked and wild.
Now they're gone, I have to move on.

Gavin Ryan (13)
Finchley Catholic High School, Finchley

Footballer

I want to be a footballer,
A footballer I'd be,
Thierry Henry, Rooney,
They are who I would love to be playing with in
Wembley,
And I would love to be in history,
For scoring hundreds of goals and breaking records,
What a footballer I'd be.

Bradley Gyamfi (13)
Finchley Catholic High School, Finchley

Crime

Every day in London, people break the law,
They will punch you in the face and kick you on the floor,
They will mug you in the street and steal the shoes off your feet,
They will shoot you with a gun, steal your money then run,
They will break into your home and steal your TV and your phone,
They deal drugs in the street and make it look discreet,
Some criminals are tall, some of them are short,
But in the end, all criminals get caught.

Aidan Breheny (13)
Finchley Catholic High School, Finchley

To My Dear Family

Tomorrow I may die, so I hope you will receive this if I do.
We're on the front line, and will be going over too.
I want to thank you, especially Mum and Dad,
For my upbringing in my childhood and youth,
Even though I was very mad.

Please tell all my friends that I've enjoyed their company
And I'm very glad they've been there each and every day for me.
Please don't be upset, I will still be there for you,
Even though you won't see me,
But you know how much I really love you.

Thank you for making my life so good
And please don't forget me,
Even though we know you should.

I love you so much and always will,
Benedict, Francesca, Kevan and Gill.

Private Genevieve Sutton.

Genevieve Sutton (14)
George Abbot School, Guildford

WWI Poem - In The Trenches

The thuds and clatters all around,
Fill your head with dreadful sounds.
Hear the men shouting your name,
Your time has come to die in vain.

All around the sight you see,
Devastation for you and me.
The dreadful smell, so, so strong,
Till you're too afraid to carry on.

Men around you, dead at your feet,
Feel the rivals' marching beat.
A loud bang and searing pain,
You are now dead in vain.

Emily Cogan (14)
George Abbot School, Guildford

In The Trenches

It's wet all around me,
I'm damp, cold and muddy,
I can't think straight,
Over the top tomorrow,
What if I die?

I won't get to sleep tonight,
I shall be too worried,
I'm going to fight for my country
And think about coming home,
What if I die?

Bombs and shells went off last night,
Shrapnel was flying everywhere,
Killing soldiers,
Their uniforms no longer needed,
What if I die?

The wounded are all around me,
All wet and bloody,
I must help them,
I will fight for them,
For my country, for England!

Katherine Savage (14)
George Abbot School, Guildford

Bang, Bang, Boom!

The bombs went off,
Bang, bang, boom!
The machine guns fired,
Bang, bang, boom!
The grenades flew past,
Bang, bang, boom!
Then we went over the top,
Bang, bang, boom!
Then there was silence!

James Clarke (14)
George Abbot School, Guildford

The Trenches

Down in the trenches I wait for the end,
The end of the fire that the enemy sends.
I cannot move, I am frozen in fear,
As a bullet for me comes evermore near.

The smell is pungent, just rotting flesh,
Once living people, now just a mess.
Why am I still here while others are dead?
I can't keep on fighting, I just want to rest.

Explosions, explosions that pervade the field,
The constant fire of weapons that the enemy yields.
The cries of the soldiers bleeding to death,
There used to be quiet, now only chaos is left.

I've been told that to fight is for glory,
But if they saw what I've seen, they'd soon change their story.
I hope in my heart that the British will win,
But the Germans surround us, our chances are dim.

Down in the trenches I wait for the end,
The end of the fire that the enemy sends.

Christopher Stevens (14)
George Abbot School, Guildford

Another Hero

A man reaches out through the mist
Searching for something to hold
As he sinks down in the bloody mud
Shouting for help as his life passes by.
He lies shivering with fright
His face glinting with rain
'Another man gone,' someone yells
But no, he is not just another man
He is another hero.

Lucy Breen (14)
George Abbot School, Guildford

Shells

Bang!
I was rudely jolted from my restless sleep.
Immediately I felt the agonising pain of the shrapnel
embedded in my thigh,
I looked down at my leg and could only see a thick, red layer
of blood.
No longer was there a roof of rotting planks above my head,
But a suffocating cloud of thick haze,
which the sun barely penetrated.
I knew what it was, I had heard it hundreds of times before -
a shell.
I scrambled frantically for my gas mask,
I could already taste the debris in my mouth.
However, all I could grasp was a fat, revolting rat.
I tried to stand up, but I could not see anything in front of me,
So I stumbled towards the light I could faintly make out.
As I hopped into the main trench,
I tripped on a severed leg
And I soon found out who it belonged to -
my best mate.
Fighting back the tears, I could just make out his gas mask,
clenched in his hand.
As I wrenched it from his firm grip and placed it over my head,
I could finally open my eyes and I realised how lucky I was.
The shell had landed very near to where I was resting,
I knew it could have been me,
As I looked around for my dead comrades.
As I stood and gazed through the clearing haze,
I finally saw the full horror of the blast.
I suddenly wondered why we had been drawn into this war.
What are we fighting for?

Oliver Messenger (14)
George Abbot School, Guildford

The Inevitable

The distant sounds deafen me,
Frighten me to the core.
Men screaming, guns shooting,
Bombs dropping,
The crazy, rapid hail of gunfire
By my head.
I wince as the shots become evermore accurate,
Ever closer.
Smoke engulfs me, I am choking.
But is it the smoke I am choking on?
Or my own fear?
My lungs are filled with dust,
My legs feel numb,
My head is being detonated from within
By the huge bangs and crashes of bombs.
My eyes close as I wait, wait, wait,
As if forever
Anticipating the moment
When one of those evermore accurate shots
Will take me as its target.
The wait is unbearable.
My face is wet from tears,
Tears full of emotion,
Overflowing from my eyes,
Crashing down my face,
A waterfall of emotions.
I pray for the lives not yet taken,
I pray for my country,
I pray for my family,
I pray and pray and pray,
Until . . .
The inevitable . . .

Megan Toksvig Stewart (14)
George Abbot School, Guildford

St Johnny

The pit is full of carcasses,
Where we laid St Johnny to rest,
He was shot out on no-man's-land,
Five bullets to the chest.

I remember seeing Johnny's end,
His wounds turning the trench water red.
But the cruelty of war will spare no man,
'Cause even St Johnny is dead.

Nobody remembers St Johnny,
He's out of everyone's head.
When I'm gone, will I be like Johnny?
No one caring that I'm dead?

Johnny will remain our saviour,
The light in our city of lies.
The patron saint of survival,
The product of the war, we've been victimised.

I'm going over the top now,
But I've served my country to death.
I'll suffer the fate of St Johnny,
Five bullets to the chest.

RIP St Johnny.

Caitlin Parker (14)
George Abbot School, Guildford

Wartime

When will it end?
Artillery fires constantly,
Rifles, bayonets, snipers, shells,
The list is endless,
Is it stopping?
Maybe it's safe to go out?
Ebony, burnt corpses surround us.

Ellen Hadman (14)
George Abbot School, Guildford

Is It So Hard To Imagine?

Is it so hard to imagine
Those years of extreme cold and pain
When we'd stand in the trenches, mud knee-deep
Always trying to find someone to blame?

Is it so hard to imagine
The anger and fear we went through
Knowing how many people were dying
Each one bringing them closer to you?

So many people attempt it
But they're time after time incorrect
Is it really so hard to imagine
This life we've tried so hard to forget?

Alice Spalding (14)
George Abbot School, Guildford

Guns And War

G uns fire from the trenches
U nderstated heroes risk their lives
N o one stays still to see what's happening
S ergeants shouting orders

A ll are scared
N erves shatter
D ust settles

W ar begins
A ll are dead
R eserves called up.

Matthew Edmondson (14)
George Abbot School, Guildford

Over The Top

Not long now, I am told, not long now
I wait in silence for my time, for the dash.
The time when all is forgotten, when all is lost and won in just
a moment.

For some time, the world seems to freeze around me,
All I can hear is my heartbeat.

Then, *'Ten'* . . .it's time, I think to myself,
'Nine' . . . I struggle to my weary feet,
'Eight' . . . yells our sergeant, his voice quivering for the first time,
'Seven' . . . I hoist my weighty rifle over my shoulder,
'Six' . . .
I nod at Jackson, sitting next to me,
I notice his chin is covered in his own vomit.

Bang!
A huge explosion throws me back against the trench wall,
My neck buckles, my back is in agony.
The flames are overwhelming, coming from just in front of us.
Jackson's screaming at me in desperation, so it seems,
Yet I cannot hear a thing.
I look around and a dozen soldiers are fleeing, over the top.

In a moment of blind panic, I follow, knowing not what I am doing,
I stumble and trip forward, burying my face in icy snow and mud,
Bringing me to my senses once more,
I rise again to my feet, and realise just what I am part of,
I feel drowned by my dangers and everything happening,
And all I can hear is a deafening buzz, but on I stumble,
Through no-man's-land.

Tim Slater (14)
George Abbot School, Guildford

The Unknown Island

The vast mountains can be seen in the distance,
Standing proudly against the deep blue of the sky
Church bells ring slowly and the quiet murmur
And chatter of the village can be heard.

Insects crawl around, exploring the dry soil, searching.
Birds spread their wings and soar overhead.
The shady olive groves stand there calmly in the breeze,
As animals scurry beneath the elegant branches.

Dust hovers above the sandy ground, then settles.
I would often just sit upon the balcony,
Gazing out at the picturesque view
And fanning my face from the humid air.

A tortoise gradually makes its way down the grassy slope,
Looking up questioningly and then deciding
That this would be the place for it to doze off for the afternoon.

Now was the hottest part of the day.
Every inhabitant on this island would be resting peacefully,
Animals lazily snoozing and lizards basking in the heat,
The cliffs tower above me and the sun glares down.

All is silent and this unknown island
Lies untouched,
With only the waves lapping softly at the shore.

Charlotte Almond (14)
George Abbot School, Guildford

Trenches Poem

I watch the youths wade towards me
And on their faces they try to hide
The loathing that's forcing them
To ignore humanity inside.
The fighting has stopped
So the screams are loud
The wounded swimming
At the feet of the proud.
They may march right back
Their job has been done
But I'm waiting in the trenches
At my chest is my gun.
I watch the youths wade towards me
And on their faces they try to hide
The loathing that's forcing them
To ignore humanity inside.
My nerves just engulf me
This suffering's the worst
The anxiety and waiting
Not knowing who'll die first.
My hunger's forgotten
As the tension keeps me awake
And as it's my turn to attack
My heart's about to break.
I watch the enemy stride towards me
And on their faces they don't bother to hide
The loathing that's forcing them
To ignore humanity inside.

Grace Arnold (14)
George Abbot School, Guildford

The Giant

(Inspired by 'The Fly' by Walter de la Mare)

How tiny to a towering giant
Must mighty things appear!

An ocean like a garden pond
Its waves like the rippling wind on the water's edge.

A cathedral like a scaled-down doll's house
A mountain like a chunky, crunchy Toblerone.

The tallest trees in the forest like bristly toothbrushes all in rows
A jumbo jet, a rosy-red robin, a lake, a great bubbly foot spa.

And skyscrapers that touch the stars
As sleek and tall as TV aerials!

Emma Clayton (11)
Glenthorne High School, Sutton

The Fly

(Based on 'The Fly' by Walter de la Mare)

'How large unto the tiny fly
Must little things appear!'
A rosebud like an oval capsule of blood
Its prickle like the razor-sharp tip of a sword
A dewdrop like a cup of water
A hair like a giant forest vine
The smallest grain of mustard seed
As a child's balloon
A loaf of bread, a mountain
A wasp like something out of a nightmare
And specks of salt as bright to see
As the sun, shining in the morning.

Rhys Turner (12)
Glenthorne High School, Sutton

The Fly

(Based on 'The Fly' by Walter de la Mare)

How big unto a tiny fly must little things appear?
A rosebud like a massive green apple
With a tough leathery skin.
Its prickle like a sharpened razor about to split hairs.
A dewdrop like a tidal wave raging,
Overpowering the defenceless land.
A hair like a snake coiling around and around,
The smallest grain of mustard seed.

Thomas Thistleton (12)
Glenthorne High School, Sutton

The Fly

(Based on 'The Fly' by Walter de la Mare)

'How large unto the tiny fly must little things appear!'
A rosebud like a hockey ball,
Its prickle like a fork spade.
A dewdrop like a swimming pool.
A hair like a monkey.
The smallest grain of mustard seed like a skittle.
A loaf of bread like a trampoline.
A wasp like a stinging nettle
And specks of salt as bright to see as a gold chain.

Daniel Cahill (12)
Glenthorne High School, Sutton

The Key To Me

The key to me is my soul
Cos in my soul you'll find a hole
And in that hole you'll find a key
And that will be the key to me.

Jamie Graham (12)
Glenthorne High School, Sutton

The Fly

(Based on 'The Fly' by Walter de la Mare)

'How large unto the tiny fly
Must little things appear!'
A rosebud like a soft feathered pillow,
Its prickle like a sharp pointy needle,
A dewdrop like a smooth flowing waterfall,
A hair like a long piece of straw,
The smallest grain of mustard seed as
Big and hard as a rugby ball,
A loaf of bread like a bouncy trampoline,
A wasp like a ferocious, mythical beast
And specks of salt as bright to see
As stars shining in the midnight dark sky.

Jennifer Smith (12)
Glenthorne High School, Sutton

The Giant

(Inspired by 'The Fly' by Walter de la Mare)

How tiny to a towering giant
Must mighty things appear!
An ocean like a jacuzzi bath tub
Its waves like a ripple in a puddle
A cathedral like a religious classroom
A mountain like a big rock
The tallest trees in the forest like a 40 foot Christmas tree
A jumbo jet like a white dove
A lake like a paddling pool
And skyscrapers that touch the stars
As small as a matchstick.

Lucy Louise Rondeau (12)
Glenthorne High School, Sutton

The Giant

(Inspired by 'The Fly' by Walter de la Mare)

How tiny to a towering giant
Must mighty things appear!
An ocean like a cup of water
Its waves like ripples
A cathedral like a doll's house
A mountain like a stone
The tallest trees in the forest like the smallest blades of grass
A jumbo jet, a plastic plane
A lake, a puddle in the rain
And skyscrapers that touch the stars
As small as plastic cars.

Lewis Metz (11)
Glenthorne High School, Sutton

The Giant

An ocean like a pond
Its wave like a ripple
A cathedral like a doll house
A mountain like a pin
The tallest trees
In the forest like the grass
A jumbo jet, a tiny bird
A lake, a puddle
And skyscrapers that
Touch the stars as matchsticks!

Luke Foulsham (12)
Glenthorne High School, Sutton

The Fly

(Based on 'The Fly' by Walter de la Mare)

'How large unto the tiny fly
Do little things appear!'
A rosebud like a football,
Its prickle like a knife.
A dewdrop like a river.
A hair like a long javelin.
The smallest grain of mustard seed
As a smooth Malteser.
A loaf of bread like a bouncy castle.
A wasp like the scariest monster
And specks of salt as bright to see
As beautiful stars in the deep blue sky.

Chloe Jackson (12)
Glenthorne High School, Sutton

The Giant

How tiny to a towering giant
Must mighty things appear!
An ocean like a puddle,
Its waves like a ripple,
A cathedral like a doll's house,
A mountain like an ant hill,
The tallest trees in the forest like grass,
A jumbo jet, a toy aeroplane,
A lake, a dewdrop
And skyscrapers that touch the stars
As a tube of lip gloss.

Jenna Poulson (12)
Glenthorne High School, Sutton

The Fly

(Based on 'The Fly' by Walter de la Mare)

'How large unto the tiny fly
Must little things appear!'
A rosebud like a giant lemon
Shining in his ear,
Its prickle like a fearless blade.
A dewdrop like a teardrop floating in the shade.
A hair like a hedgehog's spikes.
The smallest grain of mustard seed
As Mike's rugby ball.
A loaf of bread, a giant fool.
A wasp, a fierce, fierce tiger
And specks of salt as bright to see
As the stars glistening in the night sky!

Roxane Moylan (12)
Glenthorne High School, Sutton

The Fly!

(Based on 'The Fly' by Walter de la Mare)

'How large unto the tiny fly
Must little things appear!'
A rosebud like a bouncy mattress,
Its prickle like a sharp dagger.
A dewdrop like a tub of water.
A hair like a bumpy twig.
The smallest grain of mustard seed
Like a big hot air balloon.
A loaf of bread like a clear white mountain.
A wasp like a colourful rainbow
And specks of salt as bright to see
As a big white cloud!

Louise Scott (12)
Glenthorne High School, Sutton

The Fly

(Based on 'The Fly' by Walter de la Mare)

'How large unto the tiny fly
Must little things appear!'
A rosebud like a soft mattress,
Its prickle like a sharp knife.
A dewdrop like a running bath.
A hair like a rough rope.
The smallest grain of mustard seed
As a bouncy football.
A loaf of bread like the Tower of London.
A wasp, as fierce as an angry lion
And specks of salt as bright to see
As a jewel on a lady's finger.

Ryan Acquah (12)
Glenthorne High School, Sutton

The Fly

(Based on 'The Fly' by Walter de la Mare)

'How large unto the tiny fly
Must little things appear!'
A rosebud like a red, soft love-bed
Its prickle like a sharp, pointy needle
A dewdrop like a field of flood
A hair like a thick, fat log
The smallest grain of mustard seed
As small but big as a bluebell seed
A loaf of bread as a double-decker bus
A wasp like a furious lion
And specks of salt as bright to see
As bright stars reflecting off the sea.

Akeem Howell-McKinley (12)
Glenthorne High School, Sutton

The Giant

How tiny to a towering giant
Must mighty things appear!
An ocean like a sink of water foam everywhere,
Its waves like ripples.
A cathedral like a doll's house.
A mountain like a molehill in a garden.
The tallest trees in the forest
Like a patch of uncut grass.
A jumbo jet like a toy plane
Soaring through the air.
A lake like a pond sparkling
In the sunshine
And skyscrapers that touch the stars
As small as a Lego model.

Samuel Liddle (12)
Glenthorne High School, Sutton

The Giant

An ocean like the smallest blue dewdrop,
Its waves like a strand of soft, gentle hair.
A cathedral like a small village doll house.
A mountain like a prickly sharp needle.
The tallest tree in the forest
Like green, destroyed weed.
A jumbo jet, a white-feathered bird
In the soft blue air.
A lake, a cold lap of water streaming
And skyscrapers that touch the stars
As a matchbox standing up.

Melina Heather-Davey (12)
Glenthorne High School, Sutton

The Giant!

How tiny to a towering giant
Must mighty things appear!
An ocean like a small puddle
Its waves like a ripple.
A cathedral like a tiny doll's house.
A mountain like a molehill.
The tallest tree in the forest like a little twig.
A jumbo jet, a toy plane.
A lake, a muddy pond
And skyscrapers that touch the stars
As a tower made of building blocks.

Kyra Sutherland (12)
Glenthorne High School, Sutton

Keep The Line Straight

'Keep the line straight lads, keep the line straight,'
The general would say,
As we marched along our way,
We kept the line straight.

'Keep the line straight lads, keep the line straight,'
The officer would shout,
As the bullets and bombs flew about,
We kept the line straight.

'Keep the line straight lads, keep the line straight,'
The sergeant would order,
On we went and did not falter,
We kept the line straight.

'Keep the line straight lads, keep the line straight,'
The corporal would call,
Left lying on the ground are those that fall,
We kept the line straight.

All is quiet now where we lie,
As then and now and for evermore,
We will keep the lines straight.

Adam Sales (13)
Haslemere Preparatory School, Haslemere

A Rugby Day

I wake up in the morning
And I cannot eat.
I'm nervous about the game,
Don't want to be beat.

I arrive at Woodford,
The team I play for,
I get the guys ready,
Ready for war.

The ref calls us up,
We're about to start,
The ball is kicked,
It glides like a dart.

Half-time comes,
We are ten-nil down,
I feel really sick
And my shirt's gone brown.

We're near the end of the second half,
I've pulled one back, we need a bath.
The whistle is about to be blown,
We score again, the other team groan.

We have won the match,
We all shake hands,
They bring on the drinks,
We hear our fans.

David Holby (14)
Heathcote School, Chingford

Winter

S now scatters along the ground
N aughty children throw snowballs at windows
O ur family sitting around toasting marshmallows
W inter is ending, spring is beginning.

Rianna Tomkins (12)
Heathcote School, Chingford

Best Swimmer

Watching the water go,
Wishing that you could swim
With the frogs' legs
And strong arms.

Want to know what's under,
Wishing you could see,
But sadly you can't,
Take lessons like a fish.

You have to be strong,
You have to enjoy swimming,
By holding your breath every
Time you're sinking.

You want to swim fast,
In the deep blue sea,
But you can't swim
Like a dolphin in the deep.

You've got to have speed,
Like a wild shark,
You want to swim perfectly,
You've got to try hard.

Megi Dumani (12)
Heathcote School, Chingford

Lottery

L ying, waiting, always wishing to win.
O n the couch being a lazy spud.
T asting my crisps.
T aking risks with my money.
E very Wednesday and Saturday, trying to win.
R eally wanting to win that jackpot.
Y es, I have won - woohoo!

Carl Baird (12)
Heathcote School, Chingford

A Poem About A Poem

Hello, my name is Dumi
This poem is flowing straight through me
It's my first time performing a poem in front of a crowd
Hopefully while I'm reading it
You won't be too loud
So get comfortable in your seats
This is like an MC without the beats
If you want, you can rhyme along too
But I don't know when to start
Because I don't have a clue!
I live in Walthamstow, which isn't that far from here
Where the streets are dangerous and the sky isn't too clear
I know a handful of people who live there
Some skinny, some fat, some short and even fair
Now let me warn you, whilst walking down
What those bad boys call a 'manor'
Juvenile delinquents might hit you
With their spoons, hammers or spanners
I don't think it's easy writing poems
So I think it's about time I ended this poem
Because it's not that easy to think of poems
You have to think, think and *think!*
You have to think, think, think of rhymes
But I've got to stop now because I'm all out of time
By the way, I'm only mentioning this to add some more lines
I'm not trying to be comedic or sarcastic
But I really need to go, I can hear Mummy
I have to go quick before she gets drastic
So I leave you with the thought of my poem
And better get out of here, while I'm still growing.

Dumi Nkomo (13)
Heathcote School, Chingford

Tiger

In the bushes, in the middle of the night,
Animals ran scared in fright,
There was a tiger with black stripes,
Equipped with claws and teeth that shine in the night.

He was very big, not too tall,
He was the biggest creature of them all,
He had teeth that gave a painful bite,
He will chew you up, slicing you light.

Do you have any clue
What this tiger can do?
He will munch you up and make it quick,
Do you have a death wish?

One time when the tiger had his fun,
Hunters came and shot him with a gun!
They banged, popped, banged him out,
The tiger was dead without a doubt.

Adrian Shaw (12)
Heathcote School, Chingford

What To Look For In A Friend

A good friend never tells your deepest darkest secrets.
A good friend would never betray you.
Would you like a friend who did all that stuff?
A friend should be by your side,
A friend should be honest with you
And not tell you a lie,
A friend should be kind and helpful when you need it.
To keep a friend, be kind, not nasty.
To keep a friend be sharing, not tight.
To keep a friend let her know who you are.
To keep a friend don't tell a lie,
Be honest with her and be honest with yourself.

Hollie Morris (12)
Heathcote School, Chingford

Netball Championships

I got picked for the team
I couldn't believe the news,
I was gobsmacked, thrilled,
No longer had the blues.

I jumped high in the air,
Over leaps and bounds
I was so full of excitement
That I tripped and fell to the ground.

I quickly got up,
But I was still in shock,
I checked my leg for any damage,
But I only had a knock.

The next day I awoke early,
Had I dreamed being chosen for the team?
I sprinted downstairs and asked my mum the facts,
Yes I was! I started to beam!

The netball championships grew nearer,
I started to get butterflies in my belly,
I realised I needed to do some training,
But only after I had watched the telly!

The days flew past ever so quickly,
It was nearly time to play,
My friends were as excited as I was,
The nerves had gone away.

The night before the netball championships,
I had my friend over called Sophie,
She soon went and the next day came
And my team ended up taking home the trophy!

Samantha Dix (14)
Heathcote School, Chingford

Lonely

No one understood her
They said that she was strange
They hurt her and they cursed her
But they didn't know her name

She'd wander home at night
All alone, nobody cared
She'd never start a fight
Yet still she'd sit there scared

Until one day they looked for her
But could only find a note
They read it aloud for all to hear
It caused tears and a knot in the throat

'You never really knew me
So why did you cause me pain?
As much as I despise you
I long to be the same

I'm standing on the bridge right now
Staring down at the calm blue sea
Careless, calm and popular
That's how I'd love to be

So forgive me when you read this note
This wasn't meant to be
My absence will not cause any hurt
Once I've jumped into the sea.'

Holly Hereford (14)
Heathcote School, Chingford

Homeless

Here I am,
Walking across this cold pavement,
Where shall I sleep?
A shed in a back garden,
I'll just take a peep.

This is alright,
It'll do,
It isn't much,
But where will I go to the loo?

Where shall I brush my teeth
Or wash my face?
Oh I just don't know.
Where shall I have a bath?
Oh where, where will I go?

I wish I could have some toys
Or a family that cares,
Or clothes, oh, what a joy,
Or teddies like cuddly bears.

So this is my life,
Wandering the streets day and night,
No one to care for me or love me,
This just isn't right.

Anni Tucker (12)
Heathcote School, Chingford

Friends Forever

We've been friends for seven straight years,
Through the joys and hopes and fears.
We've seen each other through it all,
Even though we go to separate schools
And through all this we've been together,
We'll be friends, friends forever!

Kayleigh Gillane (12)
Heathcote School, Chingford

Colours

The sea is blue
The boat is black
The wind is cool
And that's that

The sun is yellow
The grass is green
The sky is blue
And that's OK for me

The table is brown
The TV is black
The mirror is gold
And you better watch your back

The wall is purple
The bed is pink
The teddy is white
And we have got a link

The chair is brown
The clock is grey
The wall is orange
And that's all I have to say.

Rosa Liotti (12)
Heathcote School, Chingford

The Best Friend Ever!

To have a best friend,
You both have to be loyal,
Loyal like the Queen,
Funny like a monkey,
But nice like an elderly lady,
Trustworthy just like your family,
Friendly like a dolphin,
Not like a shark,
Helpful like a calculator,
Now that's the bestest friend ever!

Charlotte Edwards (12)
Heathcote School, Chingford

Life At Home

I like baths
I like showers
I could stay in them both
For hours and hours
When I get out
I have a cup of tea
And watch a film on the TV
I like getting into nice warm pyjamas
Up comes my sister, holding bananas
I like jumping into a cosy bed
A nice warm place where I can rest my head
When morning comes
I hear my mum's voice say
'Lauren, wake up, you're late, you're late.'

Lauren Baker (12)
Heathcote School, Chingford

Forever Friends

Forever friends we will be,
Like a pair of forest trees,
Side by side till the end,
We will be forever friends.

Forever friends we will be,
Like a pair of forest leaves,
Side by side we will be there,
We will be forever friends.

Forever friends we will be,
Like a pair of paper and pen,
I will be there for you till the end,
We will be forever friends.

Waqas Butt (12)
Heathcote School, Chingford

Bang!

Bang!
You can hear me,
Maybe not see me.
Bang!
Clouds turn grey,
During the day.
Bang!
All through the night,
A very dark sight.
Bang!
A great big blunder,
What am I?
Bang!
Thunder!

Amy Alderton (12)
Heathcote School, Chingford

How To Make A Rugby Player

As strong as an ox,
Cannot get ill or get chicken pox.

As fast as a cheetah,
As tall as a metre.

He could play for an hour
And can smash down a tower.

He does not need food,
He's always in a good mood.

He is the best player
And everyone says so.

Nathan Neal (12)
Heathcote School, Chingford

Herd Of Stormers

As the cheetah overtook the herd,
The delicate tortoise flinched with shock,
Erik Elephant shook the ground like an earthquake
And Slither hissed at the crowd.

Today was an extremely gargantuan day,
Mammoth turned small,
Lizard lumbered over a rock
And Falcon turned up like a bolt of lightning.

Lion roared like a policeman shouting into a megaphone,
Pengy Penguin passionately prayed with warthog,
Dermot Dolphin soared through the water like a knife
Through a piece of bread.

The Schbunks shot around the pond,
The Schbunks were as fast as an F1 car,
Giant Giraffe pinched an apple from the terrific tree,
Parrot squawked out, 'Come on you herd of *stormers!'*

Luke O'Keefe (12)
Heathcote School, Chingford

Friends

Friends can be nice,
They're who you can trust.
You can tell them a lot,
But then again, sometimes not!
Everyone should have one,
They make your day fun.
You can have such a laugh
And act really daft.
They love you always
And should never be betrayed.

Billie Smout (12)
Heathcote School, Chingford

How To Make A Football Player

For his speed, I will take the legs of a cheetah,
Shave the fur off and put them on a treadmill
To make them faster.
For his eyes, I will take the eyes of an eagle
And make them blue.
For his stamina, I will take the boxer Lennox Lewis
And drain him of his strengths.
For his brain, I will take a clone of Pele's brain
And feed it with more footballing knowledge.
For his height, I will make a living clone of Robert Pershing Wadlow
And put him on a rack to make him taller.
For his reactions and good saves, I will make
A clone of Buffon's brain and put a special microchip in it.
For his skills, I will take Ronaldhino's feet
And teach them more and more skills.

Ricky Taylor (12)
Heathcote School, Chingford

Summer!

S ummer just begun
C harlotte and Shannon having fun
H appy as can be
O rdinary people at the summer jubilee
O ver all it's really hot
L ittle children wiping their snot
S o enjoy it while it lasts

O r be boring and wish it fast
U mbrellas up in a couple of weeks
T ans fading from your cheeks.

Shannon Markland (13)
Heathcote School, Chingford

The Perfect Footballer

What is it?
Legs like a cheetah
Brains like Ricky
Feet like Jimmy Grimble
Eyes like a hawk
Free kicks like David Beckham
Strength like a sumo wrestler
What is it?

Jon Christey (12)
Heathcote School, Chingford

Forever Youth, Eternal Life

At first we laughed with joy and happiness,
The thought of eternal youth was upon us.
We would never lose a loved one,
Cry our hearts out with despair
Or have to grow old and withered,
With wrinkles and grey hair.

Our laughter had been turned to tears.
This new way of life had caused so much fear.
Without aging, senior citizens were lost.
Their growing wisdom turned to dust.
Babies would be trapped.
Forever a child, never to say a word.

But now we're cramped, all squashed and squeezed.
No air to breathe.
No food to taste.
No life to see before us.
The world's resources gone without a trace,
All used up by the ever-growing human race.

Joanna Lyons (15)
Kingsmead School, Enfield

I'm Just A Teenager . . .

I'm just a teenager, why do I care?
I don't use the train to get anywhere
Nor do my family or friends, I'm too involved in the latest trends
Half my population's gone, I don't care a bit
It's only my country, I don't give a s**t

I'm a teenager, why should I care?
Seeing people burn for their travel fare,
I don't watch the news, Big Brother will do
I wish like them, I never knew

I'm just a teenager, why would I care?
I have no emotions I can share
Have no knowledge of poverty or Al Queda cruelty
As the Twin Towers fell to the ground, I didn't see, I never heard
I didn't make a sound

I'm just a teenager, how could I care?
I wear my religion up against my chest
You tell me to take it off because you think that's best
No! I won't abandon my faith, even if people hurt or hate me for it
Even if that's the case

I'm just a teenager, I don't care
I come home from school, had a hard day, switch on TV
What do they say? Something that I didn't care to hear
I look around and find my worst fear, just like that little boy who lost
his whole family
I stand alone, only one, just me . . .

I'm just a teenager but I do care
You think I don't know but I'm fully aware
Got my life, my love, my views, my beliefs
It is you who doesn't care how the next generation feels underneath.

Cera Alp (15)
Kingsmead School, Enfield

The Abused One's Story

When I stand, tall and proud,
Without a frown,
No one can see the terror,
Within those bright eyes.

Every action I take,
Is me in automatic mode,
All the things I do are false,
My smile, my laugh,
Even my talk.

Life to me
Is not worth living,
Days go slowly
And I can't wait for them to pass,
Life isn't worth living,
So why don't you just kill me now?

Every beating, every rape
Violates my body,
Every word and sign
Violates my mind and soul,
Nothing is mine anymore.

Every morning you come into my room,
My eyes are closed
And I wait till you've had your fun.

Can't tell my parents
Cos they won't believe
That their precious son
Would do that to me.

Danielle Yeates (15)
Kingsmead School, Enfield

Friends

Kiss my lipstick
Hold my last breath
And understand that I never wanted it to
End in death
Hold my hand
Live in me
And tell me how
It was always meant to be
Tell me the truth
Feel my heart beat
Hold me up
When you can't even stand on two feet
Be my stand
Be my frame
Wipe my tears
And take my blame
Give me a hug
Say it'll be OK
Put me in a taxi
Say you'll pay
Take me to a safe place
Take me to your home
Give me a cup of tea
Be the one I can phone
Give me a friendship
Be the one I can call
Don't leave me alone
Just be my all.

Hazel Marzetti (15)
Kingsmead School, Enfield

Mr Keitley-Webb

(Based on a true English gent)

Ah, Mr Keitley-Webb,
That is his name.
He once threw on a bonfire
A tank of propane.

A typical gentleman
With Harris and tweed
And in his five barns
He has more than he needs.

A collection of oddments
From lamp posts to baths
And burns all his rubbish
On a huge open hearth.

Five hundred paint cans
Worthless and dry,
But all in all,
He's an interesting guy.

Jamie Parish (12)
Oxted School, Oxted

Is Not Meant To Be

It's like the bird with no wing,
Or the choir that can't sing.

It's like the witch with no spell,
Or the skunk with no smell.

It's like the tick with no tock,
Or Big Ben with no clock.

It's taken away
What was meant to be

And what is left
Is not meant to be.

Chris Heyburn (13)
Oxted School, Oxted

Pick Me Up, Daddy

Pick me up, Daddy,
Fly me over the lapping waters of the sea
And the gently bobbing fishing boats.

Pick me up, Daddy,
Let me ride the sweet, balmy air
And soar amongst the whisper of the silver trees.

Pick me up, Daddy,
Twirl me round within Saturn's rings
And tiptoe upon the curdling wisps of clouds.

Pick me up, Daddy,
Let's skip through the fluttering clovers
And through waving, gilded corn stalks.

Pick me up, Daddy,
Let's sweep through the hidden, watery depths
And piggyback with a school of dolphins.

Pick me up, Daddy,
Hold me out to our natural world,
Let's share creation together.

Lucy Gorringe (14)
Oxted School, Oxted

The London Bombings

Thursday 7th was when it hit,
No one in London expected it.
People working,
Kids going to school,
Then the bomb struck,
Who could be so cruel?
Police still looking for bodies,
People still in shock,
No one knows . . .
Who did it?

Josh Elford (13)
St Birinus School, Didcot

Poem On World Affairs

The 2012 Olympics
They are coming
A lot of work to do
7 years to go
It seems like a long time
But it will go
School searching for athletes
Putting plans into action
Cleaning the area
Laying the paving
Improving the transport
They realise the Olympics are coming
Then the shock horror
Of Thursday 7th July
But as the country clears up
The focus will change
Hooray, the Olympics are coming!

Sam Reynolds (13)
St Birinus School, Didcot

The Terrorist Attack

The bombs went off one after another,
The crying children shouting for their mothers.
One day we're celebrating, then we're not,
The big explosions were boiling hot.
The terrorists have chosen the wrong city to attack,
Because when we find out who's responsible
We'll get them back.
Our capital is not weaker than it was before
This tragedy happened,
It has got stronger . . .

Richard Tyler (12)
St Birinus School, Didcot

Terrorist Attack!

Was this a one-off?
People in fright,
When the bomb hit daylight.
Tube trains trapped,
When the tunnel collapsed.
Stagecoach bus now an open-top bus,
No roof on the bus anymore,
People trapped and probably poor.
No money, food or drink,
Never knew you could stink.
Poor faces covered in burns,
Stupid foreigners.
The bomb worked a treat,
Now no more street.
Fire burning in their eyes,
The fire could rise
And London says we are not afraid!

Nathan Reeve (13)
St Birinus School, Didcot

Untitled

Depression . . . a funny word really!
What does it mean?
Killing, blood, terror . . . bombs,
Just like Thursday 7th July,
Bags . . . tick . . . tock . . . 5 . . . 4
Makes you want revenge, but is it right?
No . . . they want us to squabble, scream, flee,
They want us to be . . . depressed . . .
But if we stand strong
We will get our revenge
And it will hurt them more . . . no attacks . . .
Just carry on with our normal lives.

Ollie Ealey (14)
St Birinus School, Didcot

Terrorist Attack

On the 7th, people died
Innocent people fried
Paramedics here and there
People dying everywhere

Al Queda, shame on you
You wouldn't like it if we did it to you
Bang! goes the train
It caused so many people pain

Bang! Bang! Bang! Bang! Bang!
London was silent.

Daniel Griffiths
St Birinus School, Didcot

Terrorist Attack

We got it!
2012 Olympics
It's in England
It's been ages since it's been here
I hope I can get there

But all the happiness has died
Along with a lot of people
I wasn't there
Luckily
I'm glad I wasn't there.

Matthew Swan (13)
St Birinus School, Didcot

Olympics 2012 - Haiku

Welcome Olympics
We beat the French to get it
London 2012.

Tom Tatford (12)
St Birinus School, Didcot

Poem

Bang, bang,
All the crowd sang.

Darren Campbell was a second in front,
Mark Lewis Francis running in second
And going to pull a stunt.

Here comes the line,
How quick was that time?

Upon the stand,
Great Britain had the medal in hand.

Aaron Jane (13)
St Birinus School, Didcot

Live 8

The music so loud
So stunning
Bob Geldof is so proud

Hyde Park so packed
It's phenomenal
I was gobsmacked

So many artists
Singing so well
There was an amazing line-up list.

Nick Ingrem (13)
St Birinus School, Didcot

2012 Olympics

Olympic champions,
We welcome you to London,
Britain will beat you.

Lewis Brown (13)
St Birinus School, Didcot

Make Poverty History

Who can change the world?
You, if you try.
If you set your heart on it,
You can
Make poverty history.

While people die in Africa,
We can stand up and fight.
What will it take for them to listen, the G8?
Can it be Live 8?
Make poverty history.

A few of the world's greatest bands,
They have stepped further than ever before.
Can the G8 hear them sing the songs of pleading?
Listen to them,
Make poverty history.

Can you help those dying people
With a wristband and some thought?
Touch their hearts, make them listen,
That's all you have to do,
Make poverty history.

Cameron Stanton (13)
St Birinus School, Didcot

2012 London Olympics

The Olympics are in London, joy at last,
Seven years of waiting, I hope they go fast.
2012 the spotlight's on us,
After the announcement everyone's making a fuss.
We beat Madrid, New York and Paris to have a chance,
To show the world we're the greatest! Poor old France.
So come on London, make us proud,
Fill us with pride to shout out loud.

Anthony Lyford (13)
St Birinus School, Didcot

Untitled

The 7th July
Was just a normal day
Go to work, go to school
It was a hot sunny day
And normal for all
In the heart of London
Just after lunch
The bombs exploded!
People were injured
People were killed
London was chaos
London was in shock
Who had done this?
What did they want?
The 7th July was far from a normal day.

Luke Jepson (13)
St Birinus School, Didcot

Shark Infested Water

Open water,
Deep water,
Dark water,
Dangerous water,
Do not go in the water,
Or that
Open,
Deep,
Dark,
Dangerous water
Will be red water.
Blood-red water.
Blood-red
Shark infested water!

Joseph Kent
St John The Baptist Catholic School, Woking

Good Friday Into Easter Sunday

When the day came
For us to part,
I found it a shame
It broke my heart.

Then he got lifted
Higher and higher,
Was he gifted
Or was he a liar?

He cried out in pain,
The sky went black,
It made me think again,
He will not come back.

Then he rose again,
Two days later,
He was free again,
He was not a traitor.

I saw his hands and feet,
Marked for life,
There because of his defeat,
He will be there for the rest of my life.

Lauren Bradfield
St John The Baptist Catholic School, Woking

Make Poverty History

M ake poverty history
A ke poverty history
K e poverty history
E poverty history

P overty history
O verty history
V erty history
E rty history
R ty history
T y history
Y history

H istory
I story
S tory
T ory
O ry
R y
Y ?

If everyone helps a little bit,
We turn the caring on.
If we follow through this action plan,
All the poverty will be gone!

Siobhan Cawkwell
St John The Baptist Catholic School, Woking

Life After Death

Death is such a catastrophic thing to see
It can happen at anytime, maybe tomorrow
Look after the ones you love, mainly me
As any death can fill your heart with sorrow

To die is to feel free
To live is to keep the burden of what we must control
Dying must be heavenly splendour, pay close attention to the bee
It stings its final victim then slowly loses its soul

Have you ever loved and lost someone?
Did tears fall from your stricken face?
I think that we all know that dying isn't what one would call fun
Did you pack your bags and try to go to your happy place?

Life is a gift bestowed on you by God Himself
So don't waste the 'gift', do what you want to do
You are not just another book on the shelf
You are a person and to die is only true

Life doesn't end here
Heaven awaits my dear
So give one happy cheer
As that was your final year!

There is a life after death.

Louise McGovern
St John The Baptist Catholic School, Woking

Fairies

Fairy places, fairy things,
Fairy woods where a sweet voice sings.
Fairy houses, fairy clothes,
A little garden where a flower grows.
In this flower the fairies live,
Gentleness and peace they give.

Fairy flowers, fairy leaves,
Fairy villages amongst the trees.
Fairy wings, fairy talk,
Fairy culture upon the stalk,
Of the flower which stands proud,
With hope and love in each fluffy cloud.

Fairy faces, fairy hair,
Fairy butterflies which dance in the air.
Fairy dances, fairy friends,
A fairy bird which music sends,
Happiness and joy to people in need,
Created from a tiny seed.

Jessica Loveridge
St John The Baptist Catholic School, Woking

The Tree

There stands the lone figure of the tree,
No one to talk to, no one to listen to, silent.

Then the spring arrives and the tree bursts into life.
Leaves sprout from every branch
And begin their long and fruitful conversations.

The land is filled with colour, the tree is happy,
Children come to play with him
And tickle his belly as they scramble up him.

The hot summer months creep towards him,
As the sun bears down, his giant hands provide
Shade for young lovers.

Many people pass him.
He waves to them in the wind.

Then autumn arrives and he becomes sad and grouchy.
He loses his hair and begins to swipe at birds
With his long arms.

He survives, but only just.
He is left bald, his body left naked.

Winter proves too much for him.
His old, frail body is battered and bruised
By the wind and rain.

His whole frame droops in exhaustion.
He dies, only to be born once more next spring.

Joe Holt
St John The Baptist Catholic School, Woking

Oliver Twist

'Please Sir, I want some more,' said Oliver Twist.
They all gawped as if it was something they missed.
They asked him to repeat it and got a real shock,
Oliver Twist asked for more!
He got into trouble with some big bloke,
They treated it like it wasn't a joke.
Oliver Twist had made a mistake,
Oliver Twist asked for more!
If only Oliver hadn't drawn the short straw,
He wouldn't have been stuck with asking for more,
But he didn't even have a choice in the matter,
Oliver Twist asked for more!
Oliver was nearly hurt by a ladle to his head,
After he asked, I bet he wished he was dead.
No one could ever believe that
Oliver Twist asked for more!
Mr Limbkins saw to that,
Thinking of Oliver as a filthy rat.
The gentleman in the waistcoat wanted him to be hung,
Oliver Twist asked for more!
Oliver was locked in a dark room, (thanks to the board!)
He wouldn't get away with it, good Lord!
Oliver Twist would have a worse life,
Why did he ask for more?

Christina Derisi
St John The Baptist Catholic School, Woking

Make Poverty History

I'm sad and alone,
My tummy is empty, help.
We have no money.

I heard a loud bang,
The shelter was falling down.
Now I have nowhere.

I'm lost and alone,
We need help desperately.
Please help us survive.

It's humid and dry,
No family to help me.
No jobs to help us.

No food or water,
No resources to call on.
Please, just a little.

It's arid, so dry,
Please, just a drop of water.
So much disease here.

Please cancel our debt,
We also need food, food now,
No family here.

We need your help now,
Support with white rubber bands,
Stop poverty now.

My eyes fill with tears,
Make poverty history.
Please support with love.

Emily Buzaglo
St John The Baptist Catholic School, Woking

Make Poverty History

Thirty thousand people die every day,
Because of the money that they pay,
Kids in this world have dreams like you and me,
But cannot live them 'cause of death you see,
They are fish, waiting to be killed and yet,
They have to die slowly because of debt,
Every 3 seconds a human will die,
But all us rich folk just watch - very sly,
But even though all of this is happening,
People's daily busy life keeps working,
People are trapped like a rat in a cage,
Moving around, looking for food - all age,
8 of the world leaders joined together,
Stop world poverty once and forever,
Hopefully this will be a success
And stop world poverty in such a mess.

Bronwyn White
St John The Baptist Catholic School, Woking

All Alone

All alone, no one to care,
Lying on the street, cold and bare.
No warmth to keep you safe,
Wet tears stain your face.
Weeping softly in despair,
All alone, no one to care.
In the darkness you are frightened,
Your heart beats fast, your chest tightens.
Nothing seems to matter anymore,
Your voice is silent behind a closed door.
Nobody to hold you, to be there,
All alone, no one to care.
To people living in luxury, this is a mystery,
That's why we've got to make poverty history.

Zoe Etter (12)
St John The Baptist Catholic School, Woking

Where My Home Is

I pack my things into my case
And search the world for another place,
I climb the mountains, high and low,
I survive the arctic wind and snow,
I ride through the desert, hot winds swirl,
I search different places all over the world,
I look between the plants and the trees,
I sail on the deepest, bluest seas,
I walk along the foamy shores,
Golden sand twinkles and sweet rain pours,
I warm my feet on hot sandy beaches,
Palm trees shade the sand where the sea reaches,
I lie in the green of the forest shade,
Thinking of all the things that I wouldn't trade,
For a dirty, dingy city flat far from sun and foam,
It's not a lot, but it's still my home.

Bernadette Cross
St John The Baptist Catholic School, Woking

Bombs In London

B ombs exploded in London
O h no, I've got to run
M ega explosion, nowhere to hide
B oom, the sound of death
S omeone's mum, dad, aunty,
    uncle, brother, sister, cousin, friend

I hope nothing happens to me or my family
N ever did we expect it would happen

L ondon will never forget it
O ver in seconds it was
N ewspaper headlines all read the same
'D evastated London left in ruins' they scream
O ver 40 people . . . dead
N ever has it happened before.

Georgia Vardy
St John The Baptist Catholic School, Woking

London Train Bombings

The bombs went off at 9 o'clock,
They made streets around London rock,
Over thirty people died,
Others got badly fried,
The underground and buses closed,
While underground fires were being hosed,
Citizens were advised to stay at home,
Whilst firemen used extinguisher foam,
The news said it was terrorists,
They had a desire to kill and hurt had those terrorists,
G8, Olympics, what was the cause?
Hopefully people will have a silent pause,
To remember those who died that day,
Why did they have to die that way?

Elliott Burrowes (13)
St John The Baptist Catholic School, Woking

Fabulous Frogs

Sunlight shining, blistering blue sky,
Twinkling, reflecting part covered with lilies,
Goldfish weaving, weeds swaying, murky water,
Surrounded by a patchwork of crisp leaves.

Bent knees, webbed feet, jumps up high,
Inky, spotty, peppered back perched on a lily,
Bulging eyes poised for jumping,
Spawn like jelly, glistening, reflecting.

Croaking, groaning, gurgling, talking to friends,
The frog's throat expands and shrinks,
Attentive and splashed with spots and ink,
Moving in and out of Flotsam and Jetsam.

James Taylor (11)
St Martin's School, Northwood

The Last Hope

If only the world knew peace and not war
And conflicts were resolved through words and not actions,
If only the mind did not lash out before thinking
And take pain and lose lives in a matter of seconds.

If anger in the world had not spread like a cancer
And had not built in strength like an army of vicious vipers,
If only love could be a cure for this terrible disease,
But light must lose to dark on this doomed planet.

Brothers and sisters across the world separate into nations,
Forgetting their family lines: blood is thicker than water,
Yet as their bad will linger on as long as there is good,
So anger will always lurk while love tries to glow.

Breman Rajkumar (13)
St Martin's School, Northwood

Stars - Haikus

Studded in the sky,
Twinkling into the distance,
They shine like diamonds.

Treasures of the night,
I look in the velvet sky,
I see them gleaming.

Dots of silver blaze,
Liike glistening silver jewels,
Burning forever.

They fight the approach,
The approaching of the dawn,
Waiting for the sun.

Nikhil Patel (13)
St Martin's School, Northwood

The Worst Christmas

All the elves were running around,
Then they heard a crashing sound,
Santa Claus was on the floor,
His left foot was very sore.

'I can't deliver any toys,
There will be sad girls and boys.'
Then Santa thought for a while,
He had an enormous smile.

'You'll deliver all the games,
Here's the list of names
Of the children who were good and bad,
Now no one will be sad.'

All the elves were about to go,
Then it started to snow,
They knew they couldn't leave in this weather,
They'd simply drop like a feather.

Santa Claus had a frown,
All the elves were feeling down,
That was the worst Christmas ever,
Every Christmas has been better.

Vidit Doshi (11)
St Martin's School, Northwood

My Pet Brother Kennings

An animal boy,
A playful joy,
A computer user,
A brother amuser,
A fast run,
A lump of fun,
A little brother.

David Cussons (10)
St Martin's School, Northwood

The Four Ripe Seasons - Haikus

Daffodils in their
Yellow dresses glistening
In the golden sun

In the summer heat
I munch strawberries and cream
Sampling the rich taste

The crisp autumn leaves
Tattoo the stony pavement
Colour plagues each leaf

Covered by deep white
The sugar-coated scene lies
While snowflakes do fall.

Richard Gallagher (13)
St Martin's School, Northwood

Snow - Haikus

Gently drifting down
Winter flurries are coming
Tickling my cold face

Snow drifting softly
Piling up in soft blankets
All around our yard

Still within my dreams
Pretending to be awake
Snow melts, never there

Flushing snow flicked down
Slapping on my frozen hand
Unhappy with guilt.

James Elliott-Vincent (13)
St Martin's School, Northwood

Summer

The start of summer,
June's crystal-clear cloudless skies
And a blazing sun.

Daffodils budding,
With the sun beaming on them,
In the month of June.

People at the beach,
Eating melted cone ice cream,
On stripy deckchairs.

Cool breeze in the air,
Scent of pollen everywhere,
Summer is the best.

Sanjiv Pandya (11)
St Martin's School, Northwood

Placid

The sea grew,
Mellowed,
Rose to the occasion.

Rocked gently from side to side,
Performing our innocence,
Fell with the cradle in our rhymes.

Water resembled blood,
Flowing smooth in unique surge,
Never-ending, keeping the world, us, afloat.

Vincent Moses (13)
St Martin's School, Northwood

The War

I hear guns shooting all over this land,
I see families running with nowhere to hide.
The little girl beside me tightly holding my hand,
In front of her she watches both her parents being brutally murdered.
In her eyes, tears have filled,
Her lips trembling,
She silently weeps for those she has just lost.
There is nothing in this lonely world left to keep her.
Families torn apart,
Soldiers with guns walking about looking for their next victims.
I hear a gunshot,
The little girl beside me holding my hand suddenly lets go.
As I look to my side,
I can see blood everywhere and there she is, on the floor.
I don't know what to do or what to say.
I just start to run trying to find somewhere to hide.
An entire village destroyed,
Not another soul walks alive.
As I look behind,
I see the backs of the soldiers walking away.
Their secret is buried with those who have been murdered.
This was a peaceful land now only a grave full of corpses.
A land already forgotten,
The dead left to rot.
Nothing alive is left.
Except me.

Noorjahan Chowdhury (14)
St Paul's Way Community School, Tower Hamlets

It Was A Long Time Ago

I'll tell you shall I, something I remember?
Something that still means a great deal to me.
It was long ago.

A snowy day in winter, I remember
A DVD player, a CD player and a mountain bike
That stood you know.

I tried to jump on the bike, I remember,
I fell off the bike and cut my knee,
Crying under a tree.

It seemed the saddest thing I remember,
But perhaps I was not more than three,
It was such a long time ago.

I rode on the snowy road and I remember,
How the next-door neighbour looked at me
And seemed to know.

How it felt to be three and called out, I remember,
'Do you like strawberries and cream for tea?'
I ran under the tree.

And while he whistled, the dog barked, I remember,
How he filled a bowl with strawberries and cream for me,
So long ago.

Such strawberries and so much cream as I remember,
I never had seen before and never see,
Today you know.

And that is almost all I can remember,
The snowy day in winter and a CD player,
A mountain bike and a neighbour that stood
And me crying under a tree.

That is the farthest thing I can remember,
It won't mean much to you, it does to me,
Then I grew up you see.

Shaun Newman (13)
St Paul's Way Community School, Tower Hamlets

The Time

Life is short,
So, express a lot.
Enjoy your days,
Day by day.
Feeling and emotions,
Are all we need.
Loving and caring,
Is all we want.
Night will come,
Then we'll fall asleep.
Wake up the next day
And, explore the day.

Time will run as fast as it can,
But try to make the most of your time.

Hameema Khanom (12)
St Paul's Way Community School, Tower Hamlets

Love

Love is like a butterfly,
As soft and gentle as a sigh.
It's so beautiful when it flutters by,
It catches so quickly to another's eye.
Love starts small and ends up big,
From a shopping spree to a wedding gig.
It's so sticky yet so funny,
It's like a bumblebee with a jar of honey.
When it dies down, it comes to an end,
Some go their separate ways, some stay friends.
It can end up being sad,
But tough luck, that's too bad!

Reisha McKay (13)
St Philomena's RC High School for Girls, Carshalton

Shoes

Shoes are like people,
They are fat, skinny,
Tall and short,
Shiny, rusty,
Elegant and trampy.

Black, white,
Red, blue,
Stripy, spotty,
Multicoloured too.

Some are baring
And some are daring,
But some are caring,
Once you're wearing.

Some are sporty,
Some are naughty,
But mainly mine are just fine.

Eleanor Wise (13)
St Philomena's RC High School for Girls, Carshalton

The Infant

The baby crawls along the floor,
Like a lion waiting for its prey.
It waits and waits at the door,
To go and have a play.

It goes to sleep every night
And wakes up in the day.
She smiles in the morning light
And always gets her way.

Her hands are really soft,
Like a butterfly's wing.
She always gets a cough,
When she has her daily swim.

Daniela Fichera (13)
St Philomena's RC High School for Girls, Carshalton

Emotionally Scarred

It ain't gonna work
I don't belong in this crowd
I want somewhere that I belong
And I want to be able to go with the flow

I could disappear and no one would notice
Until I yell out from the black hole in the sky
Emotions were meant to be told
Not kept inside

Something could have happened, no eyes turned
Beyond caring
Same emotions again and again
Others erased from the mind

Stuck, trapped, not much else to be told
Forever going on, never shutting up
Totally ignored most days
I am beyond caring

Whenever they are on their own
They suddenly like me
I'm so tired of being second best
Bored of being left alone.

Kirsten Sullivan (12)
St Philomena's RC High School for Girls, Carshalton

Werewolf

The moon shines through the clouds,
Shrouding the world in its silver light.
Children run from werewolves in fright,
They scream and shriek aloud.

Madi Barwick (13)
St Philomena's RC High School for Girls, Carshalton

Bullying

Trembling with fear,
As I step on the hard ground,
Like a nervous field mouse,
I warily look around.

She isn't in sight!
What a result!
I just couldn't bear
Another assault.

I dart for the door,
Like a shooting arrow
And down the staircase
Which is long and narrow.

Camouflaging in with the school,
Panicking like a nervous fool.
I look round to know what I dread,
Bang! Before I know it, I am
Swimming in red.

Amber Chandler (13)
St Philomena's RC High School for Girls, Carshalton

Moonlight

I saw him standing under the moonlight,
The moon I saw was shining bright,
The night was cold, the air was fresh.

The moonlight shone like a little beam,
A beam of light and hope it seemed.
He walked away, leaving me,
In the cold and fresh, I am so lonely.

I will never know who he was,
All I know is he was the man
From my dreams.

Sarah Hallam (13)
St Philomena's RC High School for Girls, Carshalton

The Last Goodbye

I imagine Heaven to be
A place of perfect harmony,
But death has swooped down like a menacing bat,
Crept up slyly like a pouncing cat.

Time is still, hours pass by like weeks,
My pain and sorrow is at its highest peak.
His story was unended, he was not meant to go,
I hear him whisper when quiet winds blow.
The comforting of others does not ease the pain,
Saying, 'It will be alright,' does not bring him back again.

Standing here, umbrella above my head,
Remembering the last words he said.

Goodbye my best friend
Go and rest in peace.

'Ashes to ashes, dust to dust,'
Says the priest.

Mariah Wilde (13)
St Philomena's RC High School for Girls, Carshalton

Baby

Mewling and puking, the baby continues
Screaming and screeching like a troop of parrots, sleepless
Nights and in distress, you carry on still making a mess.

As you walk and as you talk, you wind me up like a
Spinning top. As you eat, you look like a clown and
As you sleep, you look so sweet.

As you walk and as you talk, you brighten up my day,
With your curly locks of hair, your dazzling
Eyes and your cheeky smile, you remind me of a baby doll.

So now you hear my life is complete and I'll
Treasure you until the day I die.

Alysia Haughton-Nicholls (13)
St Philomena's RC High School for Girls, Carshalton

Baby Dreams

When you were born
You were ever so small
You were as light as a feather
And as bouncy as a ball

Your eyes were sparkling
Your face was round
Your troubles and worries were out of bound

Whenever the moon and stars are set
Whenever the wind is high
You see the world in a grain of sand
And life in distant lands

No matter how big or small you are
Maybe later you'll understand
And when you do, it will be there in your grain of sand
Just wait for it and you'll be there. Just wait.

Philomena Da Silva (13)
St Philomena's RC High School for Girls, Carshalton

The Soldier

The soldier marches on and on
His boots worn down by the rough ground
And in the darkness of the night
He hears the gunshots as the enemies fight

He starts to run
Hearing whispers in his head
His heart beating like a pounding drum

His fingers are numb from the coldness which surrounds him
Everything seems so surreal from where he's standing

The sounds die down and the enemies retreat
All that is left is the silence of death
Innocent people wiped out by selfishness and greed.

Francesca Hayward (13)
St Philomena's RC High School for Girls, Carshalton

The First Stage Of Man

When you were born,
You were so small,
But now you are big
And very tall.

Your skin was smooth,
As smooth as silk.
Your eyes were white,
As white as milk.

You couldn't walk,
Not even crawl.
You couldn't talk
But laugh and drool.

You had no responsibilities,
You did what you liked,
But when it was time to have a bath,
You put up a troublesome fight.

When night-time fell,
You rubbed your little eyes.
Curled up in your shell,
As I said, 'Night, night.'

Faune Hyland (13)
St Philomena's RC High School for Girls, Carshalton

My Love

My love is like an ocean
It goes down so deep
My love is like a rose
Whose beauty you want to keep

My love is like a river
That will never end
My love is like a dove
With a beautiful message to send.

Sorcha O'Byrne (13)
St Philomena's RC High School for Girls, Carshalton

Crazy Zoo!

I went to Crazy Zoo,
The monkeys all shouted boo.

The zebras lost their stripes,
The elephant turned bright purple.

The lions went bald,
The parrots turned furry.

Oh, what a fright!

I went on a safari ride
And the rhinos had elephant babies.

The cheetahs had no tails,
The llamas had no feet.

How scary is that?

What a fun day out!

Charlotte Dulake (13)
St Philomena's RC High School for Girls, Carshalton

Bed In Summer

In winter I get up at night
And dress by yellow candlelight.
In the summer, quite the other way,
I have to go to bed by day.

I have to go to bed but still see
All the birds nesting in the tree,
Or hear the other children's feet,
Still going past me in the street.

And it does not seem hard to you,
When all the sky is clear and blue
And I would like so much to play,
But have to go to bed at day.

Ania Giemza (13)
St Philomena's RC High School for Girls, Carshalton

The Schoolboy

The schoolboy is as scruffy as a dog,
He doesn't care about school,
It's boring,
So all he does is fall asleep and drool.

He hates school,
All he does is whine
And gets into trouble
Every time.

He is as stroppy as a gorilla,
He is always glad to go home,
He hates every minute of every day
And now he goes home to moan.

He is as cheeky as a monkey,
Loud all the time,
Not bothering with homework
And this is the end of my schoolboy rhyme.

Alexandra Bradford (13)
St Philomena's RC High School for Girls, Carshalton

Holidays

Down at the beach in the sun
Playing in the sea, having fun
Putting on my sunscreen
And eating lots of ice cream

Getting in the swimming pool
Sitting in the shade, keeping cool
Lying in the sun, getting a tan
And being so hot, needing a fan

Summer's the best for clothes and fun
Short skirts and water fights in the sun
The sun is up and very light
My sunglasses are on but it's still too bright.

Lauren O'Sullivan (13)
St Philomena's RC High School for Girls, Carshalton

Dirt Face

I woke up early this morning,
I couldn't stop yawning.
I got ready for a beautiful day,
Because I got to go and meet my new school friends.

When I got to school,
I got judged by my colour.
All I heard was, 'Go back to your own country,
Dirt face . . . oi, black girl, why do you wanna come to
This school? It's for white people only.'

I turned around and ran home,
I was scared, I felt like dying.
I was welcomed home by a
Loving, caring family.

That was the end of the
Not so beautiful day!

Emily Page (13)
St Philomena's RC High School for Girls, Carshalton

Love

It is as if someone is piercing your heart.
Taking it away and making it a piece of art.
Some think it only works if you're taken away
In a heart-shaped cart.
But it's not, and I don't know where to start.

It's as if someone is taking your breath away,
You just want it to stay.
Some don't know what it is even though
It is as clear as a dove,
But it isn't a dove, it is love.

It's as if someone has covered your eyes,
Love will never leave until it dies
And if you and love stay together forever,
You'll never be parted, never ever.

Sarah Audisho (13)
St Philomena's RC High School for Girls, Carshalton

Summer!

I love summer
Because it's really hot,
Playing around,
In the sunny spot.

We're playing in the sun
And having fun,
Eating ice creams
And playing in teams.

We are eating our ice creams
And putting on sunscreen.
We're going on holiday,
We're going to Spain.
We're going on holiday,
We're going by plane.

I love summer
Because it's really hot,
Playing around
In the sunny spot.

Amy Sharp (12)
St Philomena's RC High School for Girls, Carshalton

Sunflower

Sunflower, sunflower
I love you so.
Sunflower, sunflower
Never go.
I love your colour,
I love your leaves,
You make beautiful flower
Who makes me sneeze.
I love the bumblebee
That goes *buzz, buzz, buzz.*
He eats your pollen
And goes *munch, munch, munch.*

Aimee Allen (13)
St Philomena's RC High School for Girls, Carshalton

The Perfect Prayer

I just want to cry
To see people die
Shed a little tear
Wishing they were here . . .

People dying all around me
Sometimes I feel angry
No one should live in fear
I am wishing they were here . . .

They say time waits for nobody
People waste time feeling lonely
No need to feel scared
Wishing you were here . . .

Time flies by
Use it wisely
People die with hatred
Wishing you were here

Never commit suicide
Please don't hide
I am here for you
I am always here to talk to you
I am wishing you were here . . .

Nicola Kyei (13)
St Philomena's RC High School for Girls, Carshalton

When Night-Time Comes

When night-time comes, the light fades away,
The room turns dark and shadows lurk,
But sometimes there are light nights, especially in May,
When you end your day, another will begin.

Emma Lucas (13)
St Philomena's RC High School for Girls, Carshalton

A Poem Of Love

They met at the door,
Then linked their arms
And sat at a table for two.

The candle was lit
And a vase full of flowers,
As they clasped hands and whispered, 'I love you.'

He stared into her eyes
And stroked her hair,
Her lips as red as a rose.

They looked at the menu
And ordered champagne,
Then made a toast to their love.

They walked by the water
And made vows of love,
They promised they will always be together.

His eyes full of mischief,
Admired her beauty,
Her hair as brown as a chestnut.

They blushed at each other,
Like lovebirds nuzzled on a perch
And never wanted the moment to end.

She held out her hand in acceptance to his offer
And told him she loved him once more.

Madeleine Cloonan (13)
St Philomena's RC High School for Girls, Carshalton

It's Summertime

It's summertime
This is my rhyme
Let's have some fun
In the sun

I need an ice cream
And some sunscreen
Whilst on the beach
Eating a peach
I saw a dolphin
Which had a big fin

It's summer, summer, summertime!

I really want to get a tan
So I can find a really cute man
Finally the sun is out
Let's go and walk about
The tide is in
Let's go and swim
For my tea I had a kebab
Then puked in a cab
The summer's coming to an end
Now I have to leave my holiday friend
My dad has drunk so much beer
I just can't wait till next year . . .

It's summer, summer, summertime!

Stephanie Long (13)
St Philomena's RC High School for Girls, Carshalton

Running And Running, Turning And Turning

Running and running,
Turning and turning,
Still gasping and gasping for air,
It was the beginning of a nightmare,
Getting chased,
She was finally faced.

Running and running,
Turning and turning,
Looking back in fear,
Her steps small and mere,
Tears streaming down her face,
She quickened her pace.

Running and running,
Turning and turning,
Not to look behind,
Crossing the road they didn't mind,
Bang!
Scream!

Running and running,
Turning and turning . . . that was no more.
The truck came and she stopped,
Instantly, she flopped,
Motionless and still,
Was normal until,
Her tears became rain,
In pain and insane,
She left the world with all the blame.

Annabelle Downey (13)
St Philomena's RC High School for Girls, Carshalton

Friends

Friends are always there for you,
To support you when you're feeling blue.
To laugh with on those happy days
And wipe every single tear away.

They'll help and guide you all the way,
Be there for you, care for you day by day.
The fun you share will never end,
All through life you'll have your friends.

And although there were problems on the way,
They've made you who you are today.
Your friendship is strong, the bond is still there,
You still feel that friendship, love and care.

The fun and laughter you've shared each day,
Those happy memories are here to stay.
Oh, with my friends I could never part,
I'll always keep them close to my heart.

Kate Landowska (13)
St Philomena's RC High School for Girls, Carshalton

Bedtime

'Mum, I don't want to go to bed,
There's a great big monster who'll eat my head!'
'Stop messing around and do not shout,
Go upstairs, out, out, out!'

'Just take a deep breath, climb up the stairs,
Face your fears and your scares.
Switch on the light and run, run, run,
Play the counting game, it's fun, fun, fun.'

'There's no such thing as a monster, Dear,
Now come for a hug over here,
But if you see a monster, just you say,
'Please be quiet, I'm trying to sleep, leave me be and *go away!*'

Harriet Goonetillake (12)
St Philomena's RC High School for Girls, Carshalton

My Best Friend

You can't see me
But I see you
I'm sitting alone
With nothing to do

I'm crouching in my corner
I'm living in the dark
I'm different from all the other kids
I lack the active spark

But then something special
Amazing and unpredicted
You touched my heart and made me new
As if no pain had been inflicted

So when I think of all those times
I wanted my life to end
I thank my lucky stars I found you
My best friend.

Anna Desborough (13)
St Philomena's RC High School for Girls, Carshalton

A Menu To Annoy The Teachers!

To start the meal off
There's a bowl of chatter
Including freshly squeezed slang

For the main course
A plate of missing
CAPITAL LETTERS
In a sauce of spaghetti

And last but not least
A variety of mistakes
Dipped with rude comments
And silly remarks!

Amanda Watling (12)
St Philomena's RC High School for Girls, Carshalton

In The Pet Shop

In the pet shop many cages,
One in which a lion rages.
Some pets as small as a mouse,
Resting in its comfy house.
A mysterious sense when you enter,
After all this is a pet centre.

In the pet shop many sounds,
Mostly from those loud greyhounds.
Squawking from the colourful parrots
And rabbits nibbling on crunchy carrots.
A loud sound when you enter,
After all this is a pet centre.

In the pet shop many smells,
Even if they keep the cages well.
The smell of hay and sawdust,
Different food types is a must.
A strong smell when you enter,
After all this is a pet centre.

Ellen Wilson (13)
St Philomena's RC High School for Girls, Carshalton

The Baby

The mother comes with love and care,
Stroking the baby's tiny curls of hair,
She smiles sweetly into the baby's eyes
And with a flicker, gone are the baby's cries.

Not able to talk or even walk,
So young and small,
Looking up to you so tall.

Charlotte Holmes (13)
St Philomena's RC High School for Girls, Carshalton

My Dream

I dreamt I was flying high
On a dragon
In the sky

I dreamt he was a shiny red
With lime-green scales
On his head

The dragon's teeth were sparkling white
He used his toothbrush
Every night

His nails were painted butter-yellow
Nice and bright
And oh so mellow

The tail was a luminous pink
What a colour
I'd like to think

We flew and flew and flew and flew
Until his cheeks
Were baby-blue

Soon the sun began to rise
I waved goodbye
And he replied.

Siân Darcy (13)
St Philomena's RC High School for Girls, Carshalton

Boy

There is a boy who lives near me,
I see him every day,
I think he's pretty gorgeous,
To get him, I would pay!

There is a boy who lives near me,
He does the paper round,
When I look at him,
He's like a diamond crown.

There is a boy who lives near me,
No words can explain him,
He is so nice and cute,
He is the light when the world is dim.

There is a boy who lives near me,
His name is called Tom,
Oh gosh! I've just seen his brother,
He is so nice and is called Dom.

Amilia Csepreghi (13)
St Philomena's RC High School for Girls, Carshalton

War

War smells like mouldy onions,
It tastes like sour lemons,
Feels like you're being stabbed with 100 knives,
War sounds like people dying,
It looks like a fiery death,
War is Satan's language.

Claire Raftery (13)
St Philomena's RC High School for Girls, Carshalton

If Only

If only they would listen
If only they would care
I wouldn't be this way
I would always, always share

My feelings with my mother
My feelings with my dad
My feelings with no other
Then I wouldn't be so bad

I tried but I just couldn't
I tried but I just can't
I know that they just wouldn't
Understand this chant

For they would be so angry
For they would be so sad
Then they'd know what makes me
Act up and go all bad

One day I just told them
One day I just said
'I think that you don't love me
I wish that I was *dead!*'

Cassandra Simpson (13)
St Philomena's RC High School for Girls, Carshalton

Seasons

Emerging from the dark of winter
A sleep imposed by time
The shoots push through for light
The rebirth of the spring sun
Birds burst into song

The sun is high in the sky
Flowers are in full bloom
Long days, light evenings
The sun's breath upon my face
Winter is so far away

The leaves are changing colour
The shades of autumn are in full hue
When nature shows her true colours
Darkness draws in covering the earth's face
Winter's just around the corner

Winter has wrapped around its icy fingers
And is beginning to grip tight
Enforcing sleep
On nature's tired life
The seasons' cycle is now complete.

Arianna Tinnirello (13)
St Philomena's RC High School for Girls, Carshalton

Fallen Angels

The chill of the bed crept up her legs to the rest of her slender body as
she shivered.
The tears rolling down her face like bitterly cold raindrops down a
windowpane.
Her hair so long and elegant like a lion's gracious mane fell in front of
her face to cover the tears.
Why was she here crying? She felt alone and fearful.
Her tear-stained face had once been beautiful and enhancing,
Now it was dark and distant as if there was no life in her soul.
Her tears were wiped away by her small feminine hands.
She felt so small and insignificant.
She looked out the window to the outside world.
The thunder hit, the rain thrashed down.
She was so unhappy, her life seemed pointless.
Yet she didn't know how much one person felt for her.
She never would because of how other people treated her;
This broke this person's heart seeing someone so amazing
not feeling loved.

Megan Ball (13)
St Philomena's RC High School for Girls, Carshalton

Descent

Slowly lowered into darkness.
Slowly losing control.
Slowly forgetting my worries,
Slowly lost forever.

I see nothing.
I hear nothing.
I feel nothing.

Nothing I do,
Nothing at all!

I look, I hear, I see no more,
I feel, I touch, I hurt no more,
I hear, I listen, I eavesdrop no more.

Rene Frimpong-Manso (14)
Sarah Bonnell School, Stratford

Death

Death is on the door,
You may die on your way home.
You may die in your sleep,
As you rest in peace.
You may be blessed with Heaven
Or you may get Hell to dwell in.
You may be missed for a few hours,
Then you're history.
Your family leaves you in a ditch,
Known as a grave.
Then it's you and insects, you've got to be brave,
For you will be judged on your deeds,
Which you have toiled in this world,
That's it, family gone, they have left you betrayed.

I am a slave to my desires, I lived this way
Since I was a kid, I waited for this day.
You ask me why did I live in the dark,
In the dark I had to be smart.
I tried to live in the light,
But I found the light was too bright.
I was looking for the truth,
But it was not found
And all of those years led to underground,
I was put in a coffin.
I tried to call out your name -
But you never listened.

Fazaila Hussnain Bukhari (14)
Sarah Bonnell School, Stratford

Speak To The Hand, Racism

Take a look around you and think of what you see,
Different types of people including you and me.
Asian, mixed race, black and white,
We're all friends, we're all keeping it tight.
With our colour we bring culture,
Culture in which you could take part in.
So don't fly away like a vulture,
Give us dirty looks and grins.
We don't have patience,
To live up to your expectations.
I know I have prosperity,
Friends and family who love me.
Stop giving us grief and strife,
All because you think we're living in a 'hard knock life'.
If we were all the same,
The world would be boring and plain.
There'd be no contrast, no kaleidoscope of colour,
Between me or you.
Especially if you look at it from the outside view.
If you think colour makes your judgement,
You're not big, you're as small as sand.
So you know what,
Racism, you can speak to the hand.

Barbara Omoruyi (13)
Sarah Bonnell School, Stratford

Pakeeza

P akeeza is smart and cheeky.
A little bit freaky.
K ind and gentle this lovely little girl.
E legant and sweet like a chocolate Twirl.
E ntertaining and she's very funny.
Z apping power when it comes to games.
A ppreciative in all the things she does.

Pakeeza Ali (13)
Sarah Bonnell School, Stratford

My Love!

Should I write a poem or should I say your name?
It doesn't matter, they both mean the same!
Should I gaze into the moon or should I look at your lips?
I don't mind - I love them both to bits!

I am truly like the hands on a wrist watch
As I am continuously spinning,
I am fighting wildly to triumph your love,
Because without you, my life isn't worth living.

Since the day you were born, the stars have had a voltage crash,
For, your beauty has made them look like trash.
The sound of your wonderful, soft, velvety voice,
Makes all the gardens within my heart rejoice!

Whichever way I turn, all I see is images of you,
They are gradually making me insane!
Your eyes are like two flames that never stop burning,
Which have pierced through me and caused so much pain!

The small insects are conversing with the flowers . . .
Even the clouds are playing hide-and-seek with the tall towers!
Just to see your face on which you wear that almighty smile!
That makes all of mankind fall at your feet every mile.

You must be the first wonder of the world
And the rarest diamond on this Earth,
The gorgeousness that is within you, is more powerful than the sun,
In comparison with you - even pearls look like hearth.

You are the angel that stands high above the Christmas tree,
The one that makes me feel warm like hot tea.
You have enchanted me with your glances,
They have given me the desire to take chances!

I am not enslaved into nothing but thoughts of you,
No one is essential, all our love needs now is just, us two!

Pirameena Saravanamuthu (13)
Sarah Bonnell School, Stratford

Change

Love is so confusing,
Why do I feel this way?
When I first saw you
I knew you were the one.
But I guess things change . . .
Roses, chocolates and presents
Were things I got from you,
But I guess things change . . .
You cared for and cherished me,
Valued and worshipped me,
I loved you,
But I guess things change . . .
We had chemistry,
We had passion,
We had friendship,
But I guess things change . . .
You broke my heart, I will never forgive you.
How could you?
I see other couples holding hands,
That could have been us,
But things *had* to change.

Natalie Reid (13)
Sarah Bonnell School, Stratford

The Silly Old Man

In a quiet town, in a quiet street
There lives an old man with smelly feet
He moans and groans and wails all day
Nobody understands him anyway
Everybody makes fun of this silly old man
But if he can't make them laugh, who can?
He sits in the cake shop eating a lot
Eventually his hair is up in a knot
He goes back home all alone
Crying himself to sleep.

Reena Shibu (13)
Sarah Bonnell School, Stratford

I Feel, I Hear, I See No More

I feel a pain in my chest
The blood is trickling down
I feel a rush of wind pass me
It's as if I've fallen over
I feel the pain less now
The pain is going away
And I feel no more

I hear my heartbeat
It seems to be slowing down
I hear people's cries
They seem to surround me
I hear the sirens -
The noise is getting lower
And I hear no more

I see people's faces
They seem to be a blur
I see the night sky
It seems to be fading
Darkness surrounds me
And I see no more

I feel, I hear, I see no more.

Melissa Joseph (14)
Sarah Bonnell School, Stratford

Love

K athleen is pretty and kind
A lways on time
T elling the truth and never lies
H ard-working, she always tries
L oving and caring, she is always
E legantly cleaning her bedroom and hallways
E mbarrassing but very funny
N ice and kind, like honey.

Kathleen-Marie McDonagh (13)
Sarah Bonnell School, Stratford

About Me

To me I'm the best.
To me I'm special.
To me I'm unique.
To me I'm everything.

I have one sister.
I have a mum and dad
And I haven't got any brothers.

To me I'm smart.
To everyone else I'm funny and weird
And to me, well I'm . . .

Well me!
You may not like me,
But you may like to criticise me,
I'm not going to stay down, I'm going to come up.
You're going to learn to like me
And not criticise me.

You may try to dumb me down and run me down,
Well I'm going to be smart and rise up
And drown you down into the ground.

If you don't like me,
Well, that's your problem.

Funsho Fashogbon (14)
Sarah Bonnell School, Stratford

Love!

I see you in my dreams,
Every step closer to my heart
Love is so blind,
I know we're going to be apart.

Don't leave me please,
I'll cry to death
For there will be no more faith
For breath.

You make me feel so shy
When I'm around you,
You mean everything to me,
Just like our love tree.

Our love is like a piece of Picasso's
Work of art,
You fill my heart,
With true love as it seems,
So great I could cry a stream.

For you I'll do anything,
So stay with me please
And be my everything.

I love you!

I love you!

Nazmeen Chitbahal (13)
Sarah Bonnell School, Stratford

As The Week Passed By

On Monday, I wake up, I see him,
I push my eyes out of my head,
Straining my neck but I'm forced to look away.

On Tuesday, I wake up, smiling,
Thinking it was yesterday,
I see him but something different happens today,
He stops and looks at me,
But he is forced to look away.

On Wednesday, I wake up and see him,
We walk past and look back,
But that's not the end of these lonely days.

On Thursday, I wake up a bit too late
And I hate when I'm told to make haste,
I see him, I want to look at him,
But I see my father and I know to look away.

On Friday, I wake up and it's the end of the week,
I see him and I don't even wink,
He says something to his friend,
Really mean and I think, is it because
I'm different or is it just me?

Is it because I'm Muslim or
Is it because I'm different?
As the week passed by,
I don't know if I should forgive him.

Jasmine Nixon (13)
Sarah Bonnell School, Stratford

Survival

It was dark, was I dead?
Stuck in the darkness, all alone,
I heard cries of fear, cries of hurt,
Would I survive or would I not?

My heart ached more and more,
Pain struck through me like lightning bolts,
I heard cries of fear, cries of hurt,
Would I survive or would I not?

As I walked through the tunnel, further and further,
Bodies lay on the tracks staring at me,
I heard cries of fear, cries of hurt,
Would I survive or would I not?

Hours went by, one by one,
The smoke drifted up to me as I walked,
I heard cries of fear, cries of hurt,
Would I survive or would I not?

As I thought of my family waiting at home,
Tears trickled down my cheek steadily,
I heard cries of fear, cries of hurt,
Would I survive or would I not?

Light streamed through and my heart shone,
The smoke had cleared at long last,
I heard cries of bliss, cries of joy,
I had survived, had I not?

Zahra Karim (13)
Sarah Bonnell School, Stratford

Confused?

I think of him day in, day out
His name I always want to shout
God makes hearts bond in two
Ours is stuck with super glue
I can't seem to get him off my mind
His heart is mine, you'll always find
He hasn't said he loves me though
I'm mad, I'm crazy, why love I show
My affection for him is just so deep
He's in my dreams, he's in my sleep
But does he love me? I'm just so stupid
An arrow hasn't been plucked yet by Cupid
You have to be patient and wait for your love
But I have just waited long enough
I just want him to utter, 'I love you'
Then my dreams will be truer than true
Because of him my mind is lost
My glasses and sight are covered in frost
Please tell me the truth, I cannot wait
Does he love me or is he just a mate?

Rafia Parvez (13)
Sarah Bonnell School, Stratford

Friendship!

F riends are people to be happy with.
R elying on each other is the way we live.
I t makes me glad and makes me scream.
E verywhere we'll be together as a proper team.
N o one will come to spoil our fun.
D isrespect and disputes will never be done.
S urely our friendship will last forever.
H opefully we'll be flying as happily as a feather.
I t's like being over the moon.
P eople are my friends and there's more to come soon.

Hafiza Patel (13)
Sarah Bonnell School, Stratford

The Rainforest

As I walk through the rainforest,
I feel so calm.
I touch all the trees and flowers,
With the tip of my palms.

The leaves on the trees are shaking,
All the animals in the forest are awakening.
The sound of the rain delivers quietly,
As the lustrous sun glistens out brightly.

The green grass looks so lush,
There is no sound, not even a hush.
Fruits and vegetables growing so pure,
They will taste yummy, that's for sure.

The sun has gone down,
The luminous moon has come out,
Time for me to go home,
Relax and chill-out.

Aysha Khanom (13)
Sarah Bonnell School, Stratford

Untitled

As the sands are washed by the waves of the sea
With old prints washed away, to clear the shores that will be set,
For new prints to carry on from our backward path,
As we smile and wave goodbye to them,
Prepared to start afresh.
We should try our best and be prepared,
For what we sow in life is what we reap,
With a view of goodness, or our life as a mess.
Let's not be afraid of what the future holds,
As we open the folds of new beginnings.
At the end part we decide whether we laugh
And do the singing,
For wisdom is our gift alongside knowledge,
We should cultivate both and be joyful in these blessings.

Beatrice Owusu-Ansah (14)
Sarah Bonnell School, Stratford

Terror

Terror in people's eyes
Everyone in fear
Women, children crying
Wherever,
World war III begins,
Everyone's feeling this way,
As a rotting body rots
Day by day,
Bombs being let off,
As suffocation begins,
People cough.
Bush, Blair, Sadaam,
They have no right
To play with lives,
But still they don't understand
The pain,
Until the day arrives.

Salma Begum-Ali
Sarah Bonnell School, Stratford

Love!

Hasan 4 Habiba
Habiba 4 Hasan
Between them there is no better
Their love is strong
And truer than ever
They come together in
Open hands
As if their love
Was all planned
Their hearts are
Practically joined together
They are made for
Each other
Made just for one another.

Maryam Yaqub (13)
Sarah Bonnell School, Stratford

Love!

Sometimes my mind asks me . . .
Why I miss you,
Why I remember you,
Why I phone you,
Why I cannot forget you,
Why I want to stay with you,
But then my heart answers,
Because I love you.

There are eight ways to describe you . . .
Nice, friendly, so cute, loving,
Very sweet, funny, charming, thoughtful,
In short, you're just like me!

So many questions, but the answers are few,
All I really know is . . .
I'm missing you.

Lakshmi Kaur Bhakar (13)
Sarah Bonnell School, Stratford

My Sonnet

Her hair is long and plaited so, so strong.
Her eyes are wide and brown shining brightly.
She speaks right but answers my questions wrong.
Before she goes to bed she moans highly.
She fights me whenever she thinks she's right.
Her hands are bony, as thin as a stick,
She is short but is quite nearly my height.
She races me after mosque but I'm quick.
Against my brothers we're a good tag team.
We plan our revenge in a sneaky way.
Playing each other, faces in a beam.
She annoys everyone with a loud neigh.
At times I hate her and destroy her things,
My love for her is like an angel's wings.

Musammad Rashida Begum (13)
Sarah Bonnell School, Stratford

Help Me, I Can't See!

I have got all these feelings
Floating in my mind
The reason for this is
Because I'm blind
It's like being in a cage
Waiting for someone to phone
So, I can be freed but *no!*
I'm all alone
Bashed, bruised, bullied and beaten
That's me, it's not my fault that I can't see
I feel so troubled and confused
Why do I always have to be abused?

I'm a person who's been mocked and teased
Not even a moment have I ever been pleased
I've longed to be free
And have so much fun
So, why can't I just be treated like a normal person!

Nilufur Patel (13)
Sarah Bonnell School, Stratford

A Poem For Annoying Parents

Parents,
All you do is whine,
All the time,
About the tidiness of our clothes,
Our hair,
Even our bloody underwear,
One day I will be free
And do whatever I please,
I'll have a few flings,
Get a few wedding rings,
Then I'll settle down
And you'll no longer frown,
For I will be like thee;
Bossy, nosy and whiney!

Emma Gough (14)
Sarah Bonnell School, Stratford

If I . . .

If I could fly
I would watch you from the sky
Only if I could fly

If I could sing
I would sing you a song as gold as a golden ring
Only if I could sing

If I could do magic
That wonderful world of kings and queens would
Be in my attic
Only if I could do magic

If I was really nice
I would bring you goodies and rice
Only if I was nice

If I could love
Well . . . if I could love I could fly
And be over your world, up above
Only if I could love.

Katie Holding (13)
Sarah Bonnell School, Stratford

Wrong!

You were the one that gave me my first kiss,
You were the one that gave me my first hug,
But things had to go wrong,
Why wrong for me?

Watching TV by myself,
When you could have been by my side,
Sleeping by myself,
When you could have been by my side,
Wrong, wrong, why to me?

Shenaz Hussain (13)
Sarah Bonnell School, Stratford

Our Love Is Like . . .

Our love is like a flower
It flourishes every day

Our love is like the sun
It makes you feel radiant and jovial

Our love is like a swan
Graceful and calm

Our love is like a chain
Strong with every link

Our love is like a dog
Loyal and playful

Our love is like glue
Because we're stuck together forever

Our love is like chocolate
Addictive

Our love is like water
Vital

Our love is like a maze
Never-ending.

Lena Ismay (13)
Sarah Bonnell School, Stratford

Love Life

He was just a friend
A very good friend,
But then the slightest bit more.
Now I love him, does he love me?
I'm not sure.
Some say he does, some say he does not.
Who should I believe? Who shall I not?
He comes in my dreams, I see him everywhere.
What shall I do?
Every day I pray for him, I ask God for only one gift.
Will he make me his or will he not?
Will my heart be broken? Will it or will it not?
I really want to know,
I always play around with him,
He teases me, he knows I love him,
Now I think he loves me too.
All I wanna hear is *I love you*.
Everyone thinks he loves me.
This gets more serious by the second,
I want more and more evidence,
Does he love me or does he not?

Muqadas Rasheed (13)
Sarah Bonnell School, Stratford

My Amazing Day At School

One day at school I received a prize
A great big Mercedes with the permission to drive
I couldn't believe it when I received that reward
It was super and amazing, I looked like a lord

Then in English, I received some news
That I had won the poetry prize out of a few
I went on the radio and the TV
There was so much to do, so much to see

In maths, we had a test
I had come first in the top 5 best
I told all my friends and they said well done
I was so happy that I had won

In drama we had to design a play
I was the one who had the most to say
My teacher was happy and really proud
We performed it in an assembly in front of the crowd

In French, we had to learn about going away
We were going away to France for a day
My friends and me were going on a plane
Walking through the crowds in the streets and the lanes

That was amazing, today in school
I might go again, it was really cool
I told my parents when we had our evening meal
Was it a dream or was it real?

Sophie Jackson (13)
Staunton Park Community School, Havant

The Abyss

Down,
down,
I
plunge.

Deep into the depths
of the
abyss.

There must
be an
end.

The darkness
shrouds
me.

I lose sight
of hope
and
human civilisation.

But,
wait,
I
see the bottom!

(There is no bottom in an abyss)

Then I remember,
I'm in a simulator machine.

Darren Winstanley (13)
Staunton Park Community School, Havant

Ceaseless Suffering

Oh, how I extremely despise,
Those increasingly engrossing, luminous eyes,
They draw me closer with every blink,
Bring me so far, I cannot think,
Then the boy steps in the way,
I feel so cold as I see her lips,
I shiver as she licks the tips,
I urge to feel that luscious tongue,
A sudden strike hits my lung,
Then the boy steps in the way,
My heart thudded, as she pushed me aside,
I couldn't hate her, as much as I tried,
I dreamt of how happy we would be,
It was a break from cold reality,
Then the boy steps in the way,
The flames of passion suddenly rose,
As I see her, twitching her nose,
Her bottom lip, she slowly bites,
My lust for her lasts through the night,
Then the boy steps in the way,
I see her hair, flowing with the wind,
My lust for her, means I have surely sinned,
She brushes her hair out of her eyes,
And gives a smile, holding no lies,
Then the boy steps in the way,
She comes toward me, eyes as dark as coal,
They are so deep, I can see her soul,
Within a second, she gives a wink,
But I know in a minute, my heart will sink,
As the boy will always be in the way . . .

Luke Young (13)
Staunton Park Community School, Havant

It

The tree groaned,
The white frost had taken shelter for the last time.
It was coming!

The leaves awoken,
The green jerseys marched through the forest.
It was coming!

The bear had awoke,
Its stomach grumbled with hunger,
It was coming!

The farmer was grinning;
His worm-eaten smile,
Shadowed the land.
It was coming!

The clouds wept,
For their job was done . . . they knew
It was coming.

The sun shone through the land,
Bringing new life with it.
It was here!

The spring was here -
New life and plants filled the land,
Until . . .
It was going.
It was going.

Callum Armstrong (13)
Staunton Park Community School, Havant

My Pets

I have a lot of friendly pets,
I hope they'll never need the vets.
Ebbey is a rabbit that has lots of cute habits,
She plays a lot with her ball
And always comes when I call.

Then there is Polo
Who's white like a mint,
He eats lots of food
And so I'm always skint.

My favourite is a ferret called Fred,
He's always hiding in his bed,
I let him out for a run,
He makes me laugh, he is such fun.

I have a hamster called Speedy Spot,
Is he fast? My mum says not.
He is quite old, and getting slow.
Do I still love him? I guess so.

There is one more, a dog of mine,
He's very clever and can tell the time.
He always knows when I'm due home
And doesn't like it when he's alone.
Rocky is his name
And play fighting is his game.

So now you know all my pets.
I'd like some more but as my mum says,
Not just yet.

Emma Powell (13)
Staunton Park Community School, Havant

Stormy Love

As the wind ran through her silky hair,
The sweet fragrance of her perfume filled the air.
As she blinked, the long lashes hid her sparkling blue eyes,
When he placed his hands on her face,
He felt smooth skin, no rough patch to be traced.
She stared into his dreamy eyes,
As he leaned forward to her surprise,
He whispered the words,
'I love you.'
All summer was full of love,
But then the cold chill of autumn arrived.
They were back on the hill where first they met,
But something was wrong,
The spark of love was dying,
Like a fire in a rainstorm.
Their hands touched for the last time,
For the heat of love was lost.

Michaela George (13)
Staunton Park Community School, Havant

The Cussing Match

Racism is when people say bad stuff about
Other people because of their colour

There were 2 boys cussing,
1 black and 1 white.

The white boy said,
'Your face is like a dark black night.'

'Shut up you uncooked chicken, do you want a fight?'
Was the black boy's reply.

Later that night more black and white boys came,
Also present were gang leaders Dick and Jeff.

All this started out as a joke,
But it ended in death!

Zain Umer (13)
Stratford School, Forest Gate

Our Colour

Racism is not nice and you should never make racist comments.
If you ever experience racism you'll know why.

Racism isn't good,
It's cold and hurtful,
If you felt it you would've understood.

I remember the fighting,
It was all about race,
Trading insults, face to face.

And then they gang up,
On each other,
People rushing all together.

Someone shouts,
'Give the black one a punch!'
That's the trigger
And the fight has begun

'You're as dark as the night,'
Shouts one of the boys.
'Well, you're as white as paper,'
Replies the other.

The fight started oh so small
And ended with a very big fall.

Anisha Hirani (12)
Stratford School, Forest Gate

Guns, The Non-Living Killer

Guns, guns, guns are by far a disaster
A painful way to die much faster
Just pull the trigger
How much harm can it make?
Oh you'll be surprised
It's as spiteful as a sinister snake
Guns are a firearm, deadly at sight
If ever to come across one it can be a fright
Guns, guns, guns are a menace to society
Naïve lives are being wasted repeatedly
Guns are like catching disease
By far worse than the flu
If you shoot someone
Someone else might want to shoot you
Bang! Bang! You're dead
Fifty bullets in your head
Is a tale so improbable
And yet so dependable
So next time you aim the perfect shot
Remember your attention is alone
You're not in your senses
And that bullet breaks bones
Guns, the non-living killer.

Priyesh Patel (13)
Stratford School, Forest Gate

Thinking Of Buying A Gun?

The bullet, fast as a horse
The gun, smooth as silk
Both strong as mountain boulders
But remember
They are dangerous, very dangerous, dangerous
Like wild dragons
People often buy guns
Just for the fun
They don't think it's dangerous
They think it's glamorous
The bullet, painful as a hyena bite
The gun, comfortable as a chintz armchair
Both powerful as emperors
But remember
They are dangerous, very dangerous, dangerous
Like flesh-eating dinosaurs.

Muaaz Patel (14)
Stratford School, Forest Gate

Nemesis Inferno

The beat of the music made me nervous,
As I entered the queue for the 4 loop ride,
It was time,
I hopped in my seat alongside Ciara,
Off we went through the mist,
Will we survive?

We travelled up, up and up,
We were high,
Screaming at the top of our lungs,
Oh! Argh!
It was the end,
We had survived.

Let's do that again!

Shelley Keylock (12)
The Sholing Technology College, Southampton

The Summer Holidays

Finally the summer's here
The last day of school has gone
It only comes round once a year
So make the most of what's to come

Everyone's thinking of what to do
With their 6 weeks they have free
Whether to go swimming in the pool
And which friends to see

Everyone parts at the gate
Saying, 'We'll see you in a while.'
Then Hannah waves goodbye
And leaves with a huge smile

Fran's still quiet and she just waves
Whilst the other Hannah starts to sing
Then Dani and Kate shout with a cheer
And Ellen says, 'Give me a ring?'

Emily goes with a cheery hug
As we all go our separate ways
No more waiting - it's finally here
The summer holidays.

Juliet Dowrick (14)
The Sholing Technology College, Southampton

California Here We Come

The sweet sun soaking the water from the sand,
Life is beautiful with a surfboard in hand.
Life is sweet, life is grand,
Festival music everywhere, the soft brass bands.
But everything isn't as great as it seems,
People live on streets where the hot sun gleams.
Without food, without lives,
Not having the will to stand up and strive . . .

Erin Strange (12)
The Sholing Technology College, Southampton

What's It All About?

What's it all about
When the teachers say
You've got detention
For the rest of the day?

What's it all about
When your parents get mad
For breaking a plate?
They're so sad

What's it all about
When your friends are loud?
They're attention-seeking
To impress the crowd

What's it all about
When you're alive
Living your dreams?
Each day's a surprise

What's it all about?
I just don't know
The time will come
When I have to go.

Katie Dalipe (12)
The Sholing Technology College, Southampton

Someone Special

In her dark green comfortable chair
She sat holding a smoking cigarette
And when she'd get out of her chair
If you were lucky, you could jump into it
And feel the comfort
But then she went away
And everyone cried
But I knew she was still with me.

Alice McNamara (12)
The Sholing Technology College, Southampton

Granny Smith

My apple is called Granny Smith,
One day we had a tiff,
Because I dropped her on the floor
And she rolled right out the door.
I picked her up, she wasn't amused,
I noticed she was very bruised.

Now Granny Smith is very chummy,
Soon she will be in my tummy,
I'm sure she will be very yummy.

Gemma Marolia (13)
The Sholing Technology College, Southampton

Unfair Trade

My dress started off in the ground
And that's where it grew, safe and sound.
The cotton was then made into thread,
Then taken to a factory where it was dyed red.
The material was shipped across the sea,
The dress was then made for 24p.
The dress was then flown to the UK
And there it was sold for a much higher pay.

Ellen Brawley (14)
The Sholing Technology College, Southampton

Taidi

T oo nice to be true
A beautiful girl
I love you so much
D o please rest in peace
I want you to live on.

Naomi Gibbs (12)
The Sholing Technology College, Southampton

I Give You A Key

I give you a key
The opening to my heart
Shining like a diamond
In the glistening light

Open up our feelings
With the key I give you
The key goes rusty
As my tears drain my feelings
On the key I give you

At the moment the key has sealed
Our one true love
Pick it up and unlock
My feelings for you.

Sophie Broyd (12)
The Sholing Technology College, Southampton

Marvellous Menorca

Sun shining,
Children laughing,
Delicious omelettes,
Sombreros everywhere,
Relaxing sea,
Flamenco dancing,
Splashing waves,
Beautiful coral reefs,
Dark blue sky,
Sparkling ocean,
Empty glasses on tables,
Scrumptious meals,
Grand entertainment,
Marvellous Menorca.

Rosemary Taylor (12)
The Sholing Technology College, Southampton

It's The One They Fear

Looking for prey,
Jaws open so wide,
Controller of the sea,
Following its scent in the tide!

It mustn't be hard,
To find something it wants.
Its menu is endless,
No need for fancy fonts.

Its eyes are so tiny,
Its teeth are so sharp,
Never know when it's coming,
A creature of the dark.

When its fin's out the water,
It makes it quite clear
To on-looking swimmers
It's coming up near.

They run out of the water,
It's the animal they fear,
Someone yells, *'Shark
Let's get out of here!'*

Jade Court (14)
The Sholing Technology College, Southampton

A Very Short Poem

A very short poem
About my dislike and hatred
Towards extreme temperatures
And very cold weather

Jack Frost!
Get lost!

Emily Bennett (12)
The Sholing Technology College, Southampton

Joe

I'm full of admiration for you and most of all pride,
For all the things you have done throughout your whole life,
You were there when I needed you,
To always make me smile,
For I don't know what I'd do without you in my life.

For everything that's happened this past year,
The fun, the excitement, the pride, never any tears,
I just want to say thank you for everything,
For showing that you care
And always just being there.

For all the time we spend together,
It has brought us so close, now forever,
You're not only my brother,
But my best friend,
So I shall love you until the very end.

Charlotte Prince-Wright (14)
The Sholing Technology College, Southampton

My Summer Sonnet

Summer is the third season of the year,
With holidays here and also abroad,
With sea, sand, sun and slow walks down the pier,
There's no way you can possibly be bored.

I love the aeroplanes, but not the plane's nosh,
You can go to Greece, France, Belgium and Spain,
I always go around with lots of dosh,
One thing you don't need is suffering pain.

But summer isn't always about that,
You can have fun with friends and family,
I need my suncream and my favourite hat,
Holidays are a time to act happily.

Happy times are what mean the very most,
Whether you are at home, or on the coast.

Rosy Ball (13)
The Sholing Technology College, Southampton

The Classroom Kids

(Dedicated to my nan)

Messy Mark is covered in paint,
Clean and shiny, that he ain't.
He's walking around all covered in blue,
Yellow, green, purple too.

Naughty Nora made Peter cry,
She poked her pencil in his eye!
'That's most unkind!' said Mrs May,
So Nora scowled and ran away.

Sporty Sam plays lots of games,
The end result is always the same.
He hit Greg with a cricket bat,
But still he shouted out, 'Ow's zat!'

Lazy Lauren's over there,
She's fallen asleep in the teacher's chair.
Lauren daydreamed through the test,
Mrs May was unimpressed.

Filthy Frank is afraid of showering,
The smell he makes is overpowering.
He thinks washing's a waste of time,
No wonder he's always covered in grime.

Dizzy Dianne's cute but thick,
She ate her lolly and the stick!
Once she wore her shoes to bed,
'It's in case I sleepwalk,' is what she said.

Corinne Seymour (13)
The Sholing Technology College, Southampton

Homework

Homework, oh homework,
You are so boring,
You take up my evening
And all of my morning,
If only, if only you'd go in the bin,
Homework, oh homework,
You're doing my head in.

I'd rather be with a skunk in a very small room,
Deafen my ears with a very big boom,
Eat a tarantula up in one bite
Or sleep in the desert for three whole nights.

Homework, oh homework,
You make me so sad,
Rather do all of those things,
Than the homework I have,
If only by magic you'd disappear,
If only a dog tore you up to bits,
Homework, oh homework,
You're giving me fits!

Loulsa Cooper (13)
The Sholing Technology College, Southampton

My Pony

My pony likes to eat his hay,
I like to ride him every day,
But when it's hot
He sweats a lot,
When I put the fly spray on him,
He twitches and moves,
So I have to hold him,
When it's the end of the day,
I let him out and he runs away.

Sophie Wells (12)
The Sholing Technology College, Southampton

The Vampire

The vampire lurks in the dark of the night,
To give innocent people an awful fright.
Waking up from his silent tomb,
Spying on people through the gloom.

Hiding behind the mossy gravestone,
When he spots a victim he doesn't moan.
An open window he turns and sees,
The bats before him start to flee.

He climbs up the wall and goes into the room,
Where the woman inside is armed with a broom.
He snaps it in half and traps her in,
Then sharply sinks his fangs deeply within.

He climbs out the window dripping in blood
And goes back to his coffin covered in mud.
He lies there in utter silence
And thinks of that night's gory violence.

Amy Lowe (13)
The Sholing Technology College, Southampton

The Bully

You're a bully and nobody likes you,
You make me turn black and blue.
I'm too scared to say a word,
I wish I could fly away like a bird.
I look around the corner to see if you're there,
Just so you won't give me a scare.
You say you're strong but you might not be,
You just look pathetic to someone like me.
I just want to run from your bully zone
And hope you won't follow me to my home.
Some people end it with a hang,
But I like to go out with a *bang!*

Danielle Phillips (12)
The Sholing Technology College, Southampton

About My Dog

My dog called Rusty has short fluffy hair,
My dog is a good dog and loves to dig,
When he is eating, he just doesn't care,
I laugh at him when he eats like a pig.

Rusty is not vicious and never bites,
He will always come when I call,
He loves it when I cuddle him at night,
Rusty is a big, hairy, furry ball.

I am sure he likes going for a walk,
He loves to run around and play in grass,
Rusty and I, we seem able to talk,
When I want the ball from him I shout, 'Pass.'

When his time is up, I will be upset,
Rusty you will always be my best pet.

Brittania Stokes (13)
The Sholing Technology College, Southampton

Some Friends!

Some friends
Are good
Some friends
Are bad
Some friends
Are happy
Some friends
Are sad
Some friends
Are understanding
Some friends
Get mad
But one thing's for sure
Now you will see
Not all friends are as special as you are to me.

Lily Fitzgerald (12)
The Sholing Technology College, Southampton

I Wish

I wish I could die today
Instead of wondering with every breath I take
If you were ever there for me
Or if all we did was just for you

I wish I could cry today
Instead of bottling up everything I feel
Staring stone-faced at the ceiling
While my heart breaks on the floor

I wish I could scream today
Instead of looking at your picture
Trying to guess what you were thinking
Resolved to love your memory

I wish I could hate today
Instead of hurting from your words
Listening to the songs you like
Wishing it was you speaking

I wish I could erase every thought
Instead of seeing you in bed with her
Entwined and entranced in the heat of passion
Not seeing me standing pale at the door

I wish I could keep you with me
Instead of burning everything you left
Ignoring your quickly pleaded excuses
Slamming the door as I slam shut my heart

I wish upon a shattered star
As the little pieces fall to the ground
Too small to put back together
It fades, I fade and you haunt my mind

The last thing that I am, I was, but never again will be is whole.

Sian Edwards (13)
The Sholing Technology College, Southampton

The Ship

Aboard the ship were the crew,
Visitors and tourists were welcome too.
'All aboard,' the captain shouted.
When everyone had boarded the ship
We finally set sail around the world.

I wander around my cabin,
Making myself at home.
Placing photos here and there,
I walk through the narrow walkways.

The bell rings, time for lunch,
Everyone gathers and settles down.
Waiters bring out the food,
People can't wait to tuck in.
However, I just sit there all alone,
Wanting to go back home to see all my family.

Hours later we go to bed.
I can't sleep and I hear a big bang.
I get up and go up on deck.
I see big clumps of ice scattered around.
Looking towards the sea, oh no, icebergs,
I turn round and see everyone behind me.

The ship starts to sink.
There are not enough lifeboats for everyone.
So people jump out into the freezing cold sea.
My heart beats so fast.
I finally get on the last lifeboat.
Only a couple of hours have passed.
The ship has sunk. Why did I come?
Memories will always stay in my head,
Of that terrible night.

Sandra Shotter (13)
The Sholing Technology College, Southampton

Love

Why does love hurt?
Make your heart bleed?
You're head over heels,
There's nothing you need.
Then along comes someone else
And takes your love away,
You're back to square one,
Yet another day.
You wanted him bad,
You thought he was yours,
A family, kids,
But now your heart pours.
He ran away,
Found something more,
Leaving your heart
Empty and sore.
You mope around,
Think of nothing else,
About your dream family,
A sports car, a house.
Just forget about him,
He lost out,
He's wishing for you back,
Without a doubt.
You'll find someone better,
Have your big day
And new love will be faithful
In every way.
Just leave him not knowing what might have been,
What you might have done, missed or seen.

Danielle Lebbern (13)
The Sholing Technology College, Southampton

Defeat Wars

If the world had no socks
Our feet would get cold
And if our feet got cold
Our feet would fall off
And if our feet fell off
We wouldn't be able to walk
And if we couldn't walk
We couldn't exercise
And if we couldn't exercise
We would get fat
And if we got fat
We would become lazy
And if we were lazy
We would have no leaders
And if we had no leaders
We would have no wars!
So the way to defeat wars
Is to get rid of socks!

Hazel Atkins (12)
The Sholing Technology College, Southampton

I Hate You

Y ou make me sick,
O bviously you're
U nmistakenly fat,
R eally stupid and
E ver so

M ean to me.
Y ou never get

M e anything
A nd are always really
T ight, I'll hate you for
E ternity.

Jennifer Rymer (13)
The Sholing Technology College, Southampton

A Child's Unwanted Voice

I don't have a voice,
I never have a choice,
No one ever listens to me.

I try to say
Things every day,
But the leaders don't hear me.

When I try to speak,
Each and every week,
You don't notice me.

And when I talk,
You just go and walk,
It's not fair really.

I want to be heard,
I want to say a word,
So you better listen to me!

Alannah Knowles (12)
The Sholing Technology College, Southampton

My Way

The blood on my hands,
The sweat on my face,
The dagger on the floor,
What a disgrace!

I feel betrayed,
I feel confused,
What have I done?
I feel so used!

I felt so powerful,
I felt so sly,
She was my enemy,
She had to die!

Tiffany Bray (12)
The Sholing Technology College, Southampton

Baby Bliss

Drooling,
Bawling,
Sucking dummies,
Crying for their mummies,
Wearing a nappy,
Making them unhappy,
But they soon grow out of this,
Baby bliss.

Now crawling,
Still bawling,
Teething gums,
Maybe sucking their thumbs,
It looks like it's raining,
But they're just potty training,
But they soon grow out of this,
Baby bliss.

Lauren Clark (11)
The Sholing Technology College, Southampton

A Best Friend

A best friend is someone
Who is always there for you
Who is caring and understanding

A best friend is someone
Who gives you hugs
And helps you when you are feeling down

A best friend is loving
And funny to be with

But the best thing about friends
Is they last forever.

Sherrilee Burnett (12)
The Sholing Technology College, Southampton

Weather

Weather makes me glad
When it's sunny and hot
Weather makes me smile
When it's raining and cold

Whether the weather is hot
Whether the weather is cold
Both makes me happy
In sunshine or snow.

Stephanie King (13)
The Sholing Technology College, Southampton

Teachers

Teachers
They always give you detentions
For not doing homework
Teachers
I think they sit at home
And think of ways to make us suffer
Teachers
Who needs 'em?

Verity Bray (12)
The Sholing Technology College, Southampton

Commemoration Day

A day to remember the pain
And torment that others went through.
To remember the brave and courageous,
To remember those who fought for our country.
To remember those at home who endured the hardships,
To remember and celebrate the day of our victory in Europe
And all of the people that made us who we are today,
Us that live in freedom, with pride.

Katherine Hibdige (14)
The Sholing Technology College, Southampton

A Hole In My Heart

There's a hole in my heart that needs repair.
It came to me when the affair was found.
The one I cherish I thought wouldn't dare,
I thought he was so unbreakably bound.

He found his love when he was led astray,
She was a good friend till we fell apart.
My love was burnt and made me run away,
I lost my innocence, faith in my heart.

He was so important in my life,
I believed my great love had just begun.
The jagged hole was made with a sharp knife,
My life was just finished, my life was done.

When we split up he was the one that I missed,
Maybe one day he will bring back a kiss.

Jade Wyse (13)
The Sholing Technology College, Southampton

No Matter Of Life And Death

Walking by the river but at what cost?
She got hypothermia, she was cold.
She was disorientated and lost,
At only 18 she looked pinched and old.

We could have lost her but she then survived,
Our lives would be blighted with only regret.
She could have died but she was revived,
We were upset but we couldn't forget.

What the ambulance crew did for us all,
Quick and efficiently they pumped on her chest.
They saved her life about four times or more,
Then the doctors told her she had to rest.

This could have been a real catastrophe,
But life and hope can overcome tragedy.

Hannah Fox (13)
The Sholing Technology College, Southampton

Love

Love is like a rose, it is beautiful.
Love is like the sun, it lasts forever.
Love is like a handbag, it is useful.
Love will then always keep us together.

Love is like a maze, there are lots of doors.
Love can start at any time of your life.
You may have wars but you just need a pause.
Love can sometimes hurt, it is like a knife.

Love will last long, you've just got to help it.
Love is a feeling, never goes away.
Love will come soon, don't worry about it.
Love will then last all day and every day.

So just remember, love will soon find you
And when it does, you will be stuck like glue.

Lucy Bowers (12)
The Sholing Technology College, Southampton

Death Of Nan

She has gone from me, she was my best friend,
She is in Heaven to be with her pet.
So now my heart, I know it will not mend,
She walks in Heaven, I'll never forget.

My heart has broken like a china doll,
Only memories and thoughts of my nan.
I can remember when we used to stroll,
When she would cool herself down with her fan.

She was a remarkable caring girl,
She used to have lovely golden blonde hair,
Beautiful sun-kissed mane, riotous curls
And she used to give me much love and care.

Nan, if you can hear me, now I love you
And I know you love the dogs and me too.

Carla Swanborough (13)
The Sholing Technology College, Southampton

Unique

Our love is like an obsession to me
I thought love was like the horrible plague
I thought 'in love' I was ashamed to be
Such a fool I was to think it was for real

What a fool, I was to be deceived
What a fool, I have been badly betrayed
What a fool, my heart has lost its love key
My love has no need for me anyway

Now you have left, there are no more bad lies
Now you have left, I have no more beauty
Of your freckled, pale face with bright blue eyes
Now you have left, I cannot see my cutie

No pain, no gain, if I don't have a peek
I believed that our love was unique.

Rukudzo Munetsi (13)
The Sholing Technology College, Southampton

Boy Next Door

The new boy next door has moved in today,
I can't help but think of him all the time,
I'm hoping that he doesn't go away,
He is so fine, I wish he could be mine.

He is thirteen and his name is Daniel,
Every time I see him he makes me blush,
He looks at me with eyes of a spaniel,
It might just be a temporary crush.

The way he walks, he is so very sweet,
I hope that his mother likes me because,
When we're together I feel so complete,
When we are together I get a buzz.

I need some help, I don't know what to do,
I just want to say to him, 'I love you.'

Naomi Jerrim (13)
The Sholing Technology College, Southampton

When In Love

When you're deeply and magically in love,
You will always dream about your first kiss.
Being in love sends you far up above,
Give him a hug and you're his little miss.

When you're not with him you get heartache,
But you'll always give him ten out of ten.
You will hope that you two will never break,
Thinking that you'll never see him again.

Your love has the beauty of a sweet dove,
You like to sparkle like a shiny star,
You're loving the fun that lives in your love,
You're hoping your relationship goes far.

You're now sitting at home really upset,
You're regretting the person that you met.

Pam Barrett (13)
The Sholing Technology College, Southampton

My Love For You

My love for you is like a summer's day,
It is blazing hot like the summer's sun.
It is everlasting, that's why you stay,
But believe me it's only just begun.

Seeing you today lightens up my face,
This feeling makes me never want to part.
Like the way that you talk when we embrace,
This is the best feeling to me sweetheart.

If we ever part, it's you I will miss,
Like in the morning you don't want to leave,
But before you do, you give me a kiss,
I trust you when you say, 'I won't deceive!'

If you go, I shall miss you forever,
I think we are forever together.

Abby Kilbane (13)
The Sholing Technology College, Southampton

Secret Man

He's my secret man who I like a lot
He likes me too, I'm really confused
When he walks past me, I feel really hot
If he talks to a girl, I feel quite used

But my secret man I think he is all mine
He likes dance, hip hop and fast R&B
When he kisses me I feel on cloud nine
I love him a lot and know he loves me

I really miss him now we are apart
I really love him, my feelings are strong
He loves me too, he owns my beating heart
When I think of him my heart sings a song

I love him, he is my childhood sweetheart
Nothing, not ever, could keep us apart.

Lauren Duer (13)
The Sholing Technology College, Southampton

My Best Friend

Sitting in my room, thinking of my past,
Thinking of my pet, my conscience, my friend,
The life we had together did not last,
My heart from within, I know I will not mend.

He was my little baby, only four,
Or if you prefer dog years, twenty-eight,
I know I could not love him any more,
But to tell him now, it is much too late.

From when we took him in, from his first home,
He was strong and proud like a black stallion,
But sometimes just scared of a garden gnome,
Yet even so, he was my companion.

Bodey, if you can hear me now, I love you
And in my heart, I feel you love me too.

Natasha Smith (13)
The Sholing Technology College, Southampton

Love

If you're in love, it is bliss,
You share everything with your sweetheart,
Even give him on the lips a kiss,
But now you both are apart.

Love is around you everywhere you go,
People holding hands with their lover,
But there's one thing that he didn't know,
That you would never leave him for another.

Just forget that he cared
And brought you all those things
And all the things you both shared,
But all you wanted was a wedding ring.

You did everything together,
But now he's lost forever.

Nicola Jones (13)
The Sholing Technology College, Southampton

Love

Is the one I love, a friend or a crush?
Could he and I be true, or just pretend?
When I see him at school, he makes me blush,
If it is real, it could last 'til the end.

When he talks, I feel light as a feather,
I love the way his face makes my heart race.
The sound of his voice, I'll know forever,
The way he moves makes me want to embrace.

When we're together, I feel so complete,
When we're together, we have so much fun.
He's so great, how can anyone compete?
My love for him has only just begun.

When we're together, I feel utter bliss,
I can't wait, until we have our first kiss.

Sophie-Fern Jarvis (12)
The Sholing Technology College, Southampton

Weather!

The sun is shining
The weather is bright
At night-time it's chilly
So I could get frostbite

The trees are swaying
The floor is dirty
The twisters are windy
The hailstones just hurt!

Laura England (12)
The Sholing Technology College, Southampton

Weather!

The sky is blue
So I can see you
The clouds are grey
So I had to stay
The sun is shining
The sky is clear
The trees are rustling
And the birds are chirping.

Chloe English (12)
The Sholing Technology College, Southampton

Winter And Summer

Cold, hot,
Snow, heat,
Boiling, freezing,
Fun, boring,
Cloudy, sunny,
Raining, sweaty,
Skiing, beach,
Winter, summer.

Megan Llewellyn (12)
The Sholing Technology College, Southampton

I Love You, Mum

I love you Mum and I always will do,

L ife won't be the same if you weren't there every day,
O ver the past years
V ery special things have happened.
E specially between me and you.

Y ou don't know how much I love you,
O ther people don't know either,
U make me feel so happy.

M um, I can't bear being away from you,
U are a true mum to me and always will be,
M um, I love you, I honestly do!

Naomi Holloway (11)
The Sholing Technology College, Southampton

Grandad!

G reatest grandad ever
R eally cuddly
A super Saints fan
N ever gives up
D efinitely the best
A lways in my heart
D reaming of you always.

Georgie Brown (12)
The Sholing Technology College, Southampton

Nanny

N ever forgotten
A lways there for me
N an, I love you, I hope you love me
N oble and wise
Y ou're always in my heart.

Clare Jauncey (12)
The Sholing Technology College, Southampton

My Secret Lover

My secret lover cannot stay away,
He wants me to be his only sweetheart,
I see him outside school every day,
I really wish we could make a good start.

It would be good if I just knew his name,
I don't have the nerve to walk up to him,
His and my humour is almost the same,
He makes me feel weak in every limb.

It would be fantastic if we would walk,
I really hope he never goes away,
It would be better if we could just talk,
But I have a feeling that he will stay.

My secret lover is so fit and fine,
My secret lover is so good and kind.

Laura Carter (13)
The Sholing Technology College, Southampton

Love

Love is something great, you don't like to hide
Everyone enjoys it once in a while
And if you say, 'I love you,' no one will mind
Once you have someone's love, you always smile
You feel lucky to have a man so kind
Who loves and adores you for who you are
Who is lovely and always on your mind
You think of him as the best football star
Then one day you wake up and he's not there
You feel like the whole world has ended
The thought of him leaving you cannot bear
The pain you feel will never be mended
Do not worry, you'll find another man
If you look in your heart, you know you can.

Hannah Bowler (12)
The Sholing Technology College, Southampton

Love

Love is fantastic and really special,
Love is a feeling I never forget,
Love's expression will never be glacial,
Love is something you will never regret.

Love is what you want to keep forever,
So you can make a strong relationship,
Stay with the person you love, together,
Have fun with them whatever the weather.

The love you share might last all of your lives,
You feel special together all the time,
If you're ready, become husband and wife,
Then love is like a very special bind.

Hopefully to spend all your life together,
Stay together forever and ever.

Rebecca Gilbank (13)
The Sholing Technology College, Southampton

Love!

My boyfriend has dumped me leaving heartbreak,
I still remember the first time we kissed,
I wake up later, my heart starts to ache,
I'll remember all the good times I'll miss.

These stupid feelings called love and despair,
They seem to mess around in my small head.
But if he still loved me I'd know he cared
And now I just lie on my lonely bed.

The first time I met him my love just grew,
I'll still love him forever and ever,
Now we are over and totally through,
But now I wish we were back together.

Later that day I had the longed-for call,
Back together, the best present of all.

Lorna Wynn (13)
The Sholing Technology College, Southampton

Death

You and I are meant to be together
It was only last week that we did wed
I thought our love, it would last forever
I walked in and saw you lying there, dead

I saw you laying there, no it is not true
I thought and hoped that you were here to stay
You must remember I'll always love you
We have a precious baby on the way

You were a brilliant father-to-be
Tonight I was going to break the news
I wished and hoped you would be here with me
Now all I'm to celebrate is the blues

Goodbye dearest and everlasting love
See you again when I die, up above.

Emma Wright (12)
The Sholing Technology College, Southampton

Love

I love you so much, you grow in my heart
You'll always be there, even when you die
I knew that it would be you, right from the start
We'll always be true, never tell a lie

It will be just you, me and the children
In our own small cottage, no one shall know
And we shall have fun again and again
We will never be feeling sad or low

My love for you is forever glowing
It doesn't matter what sort of weather
We will always be there for each other
Our love will be strong and will always grow

Because I will love you through my lifetime
And forever and ever you'll be mine.

Helen Wilcox (13)
The Sholing Technology College, Southampton

Love

I know that all I have for you is love,
But you look at my face and go away,
You are like an angel from above
And I always think of you night and day.

Then you come to me with your eyes aglow
And still today I remember that kiss,
Then your beauty makes my heart swell and grow
And I know it is you that I will miss.

My love for you, I know you would agree,
Is a unique thing I must surely share,
Even though some people would disagree,
Losing your love is more than I could bear.

This will be tough for our parents to take,
But if I left you, my full heart would break.

Jennifer White (13)
The Sholing Technology College, Southampton

Death By Beer

Lonely, he was so cold, cold and icy,
The loss of this man made me shed a tear,
He was looking faded, not worth a price,
When I saw him, the sight filled me with fear.

He made not a sound, not even a peep,
Not a murder weapon, only the beer,
All alone he had drunk himself to sleep,
The fun had gone, there wasn't any cheer.

No one was around, no one to be seen,
I heard someone creeping up and down stairs,
Someone had long gone, they had left the scene,
He looked so helpless, not even a care.

I left him all alone, he did not fear,
I don't care; it was he who drank the beer.

Danielle Smethurst (13)
The Sholing Technology College, Southampton

Love

My heart belongs to him, the boy I love,
He is very kind and always helpful,
When I see him, I float up like a dove,
Promises he keeps, he's never doubtful.

When he talks I feel light as a feather,
When he smiles at me I just start to blush,
I wonder if we will be together?
I hope that it is more than just a crush.

When we're together I feel so complete,
When I'm down he always lights up my life,
He's always caring and ever so sweet,
I hope that we become husband and wife.

I can't wait until our very first kiss,
When I am near him I feel utter bliss.

Lucy Gray (12)
The Sholing Technology College, Southampton

Nature Is So Silent

Every day wind swiftly blows our hair,
In nature, it is often so silent.
It can be so peaceful but always bare
And sometimes we hear wind being violent.

Every night we see it all so dark,
At the time we might see creeping insects.
As they all hide beneath the crispy bark,
Log lifts - you never know what to expect.

The wind is there all day and in the noon,
It just rustles through all the piles of leaves.
At nine o'clock out comes that shiny moon,
When the day is all over, the sun leaves.

We look at all those trees, fir, oak and pine,
Then I just wish that all nature was mine.

Claire Medcalf (13)
The Sholing Technology College, Southampton

Death

When I found her in a great lake of blood,
Her body was lifeless, all freezing cold,
Her perfect young face was covered, dark red,
What a shame she was only ten years old.

On her perfect face was the look of fear,
She must have frozen herself to death,
All I could do was sigh and shed a tear,
She was lying there still not taking a breath.

Next to her was a knife covered in blood,
In her wrist were several slits, bleeding,
Is there a reason in the stars above?
Now I am sitting alone here grieving.

We thought our love would last forever,
Now she has left me, but gone to Heaven.

Ellis Hawkins (13)
The Sholing Technology College, Southampton

The Weather

The weather is a big part of our lives,
It helps us plan what to do day to day,
Men use it to plan a day with their wives,
People listen to what forecasters say.

A day at the seaside is so much fun,
You can wear bikinis and eat ice creams,
Children get soaked, using their water guns,
I love to play games on the beach in teams.

The ground is so slippery when it rains,
Rainy days stop people from going out,
When it rains hard the world starts to complain,
Children aren't happy so they start to shout!

The thunder roars, which makes the children scream,
When it snows, rosy faces start to gleam.

Erin Foster (13)
The Sholing Technology College, Southampton

Because Of One Girl!

Because of one girl, I felt ill.
Because of one girl, I was still.
Nobody cared and nobody will,
My mind was raging, with the word kill.
I'm not on my own, I have my mum.
She says to me, 'I know what will come.'
Now I'm lying down in a bed,
Ready to say goodbye and be dead.
So why did I have to kill myself?
Because of one girl's big nasty mouth.

Amy Taylor (12)
The Sholing Technology College, Southampton

Nanny

You help me up when I fall down,
When I'm sad, you'll be my clown.
When I'm ill, you'll comfort me,
Round your house, I'll always be,
Up, down, all around,
Keeping my feet on the ground,
Best friends we are, you and me,
You're the best, you're my nanny.

Amy Skelton (12)
The Sholing Technology College, Southampton

Friends

Big, small, tiny, tall,
They are great friends after all.
They keep you out of danger,
When you are around a stranger,
What more could you ask for
But friends?

Catherine Saunders (12)
The Sholing Technology College, Southampton

Love

Love is reflected in different ways,
Your heart beats faster, you can imagine,
You can't stop loving them for one brief day,
You feel you could enter a pageant!

You feel you could just grow old together,
You would do anything for your one love,
Stay together no matter the weather,
Love is just like a gift sent from above!

When you've finally found love you will know,
You go weak at the knees and maybe shy,
It's a strong feeling that will never go,
It will hurt you the day you say goodbye!

This precious, vast love is all around you,
Always there even though you never knew!

Gemma Dashwood (13)
The Sholing Technology College, Southampton

Mums Are Mayhem!

When Mum gets ready to go out,
You wouldn't believe, I don't scream and shout.
I'm sat on the sofa for over an hour,
While she has a very long shower.
She straightens her greasy black hair
And thinks very hard about what to wear.
When she's finally ready to go,
It's winter already and started to snow.
A snow drop lands upon her dress,
She shouts, 'Oh no, I look a mess.'
Then she has to get changed again,
How many hours? Probably 10!

Charlotte Day (12)
The Sholing Technology College, Southampton

Fire

Fire made by man used by man all around
For many different reasons, good and bad
Upsetting people, cheering on the in and outside
Fire, powerful, a monster destroying anything in its sight
Cremating anything that gets in its way, killing and destroying

Wood and wood mixed together, power used
Strong arms needed, very fast quick movement
Rubbing, rubbing, takes a long time, speed is needed to
make a flame
Puff of smoke, blow, blow, makes a flame
Campfires need these, people chant around it happily

Matches lit, be careful, dangerous, a safety hazard like an illness
It strikes again and again until no more can be taken
Things burnt when dropped it looks for a gullible material
It pounces on it and covers it completely until only burnt strips are left
It turns to its next victim

Flame, add material in a house, *fire*
It spreads like butter from material to material
The family awakes by constant beeping, it's the *fire alarm*
Coughing, panicking, puzzled what to do, gas is an army
invading their lungs
Fire getting bigger and bigger, fire engine coming, too late,
the bodies burnt

Fires make people's bodies and souls warm
Sometimes it is too hot, things catch alight
Lit match put it out, quickly, quickly, could spread, dangerous
Water is fire's biggest enemy
It kills it, that is what fire is scared of

Fire made by man used by man all around
For many different reasons, good and bad
Upsetting people, cheering people on the in and outside
Fire, powerful, a monster destroying anything in its sight
Cremating anything that gets in its way, killing and destroying.

Danielle Maunder (13)
The Sholing Technology College, Southampton

Bullies

Finally, school's over at last,
What happened this week is all in the past.

On Monday they pulled my hair,
They wouldn't get off me, they just didn't care.

On Tuesday they called me nasty names,
They also tripped me up in games.

On Wednesday they pushed me over at play,
They kept threatening me for the rest of the day.

On Thursday they stole my money for a drink,
They then threw my planner in the science room sink.

So finally it's Friday, I can't tell anyone what's going on,
It's been going on for weeks.
I'm so sad,
But they will get mad,
If I mention it to anyone.

Laura Price (12)
The Sholing Technology College, Southampton

On The Loo

So I was sitting on the loo one day,
A thought just missed my head.
My French homework all over the floor,
If it ain't finished I'm dead.

So I wiggle around, on the loo I am,
A thought squeezed into my head.
What if a thought had just missed me,
Maybe 'twas something I'd dread.

So I pick up a book, on the loo still I am
And an 'if' came into my head.
'If that thought that missed is still waiting around,
I shall go catch it,' I said!

Ellie Cove (12)
The Sholing Technology College, Southampton

People Poem

There once was a man named Don,
He was a lying, cheating con,
His wife found out and started to shout,
Next time you looked, she was gone.

There once was a woman called Jill,
She married a man called Bill,
They walked up the aisle, with a great big smile,
But soon they were killed by Will.

There once was a man called Jim,
He was extremely dim,
He juggled with knives and lost his lives,
And that was the end of him.

There once was a witch called Mary,
She was extremely scary,
She cast a spell to send people to Hell,
She definitely wasn't a fairy.

There once was a girl named Molly,
She had a rather big dolly,
The dolly was evil, there was such an upheaval,
Then dolly ate Molly and Polly.

There once was a girl called Ellie,
Who liked to watch the telly,
She sat there all day, eating away
And ended up with a big belly.

Emily Hamilton-Peach (13)
The Sholing Technology College, Southampton

Different But Equal

'Hi, Tasmin, how was your day?'
'OK, Mum, it wasn't too bad.'
But that's not true, that was a lie,
It was the worst day I've ever had.

They spat at me as I walked by
And stuck gum in my hair.
They stole my trainers in PE
And pushed me down the stairs.

They called me names in geography
And stabbed me with a pen.
They ripped up my maths homework,
So I got a detention, again.

They egged me as I walked back home
And broke my brand new bag.
They branded me a 'stupid chink',
'Scum', 'a dirty slag'.

They sent me another text message,
My fourth death threat this week.
I know these people are serious,
But I'm frightened to stand up and speak.

These racist girls have ruined my life
And filled my days with fear.
So now it's time to end the life
Of Tasmin Orkasheer.

Danielle Tugby (13)
The Sholing Technology College, Southampton

The Footballer

There once was a boy who had a dream to manage a football team,
He had a plan,
He asked a man,
The man said, 'You need a routine.'
The boy said, 'What do you mean?'
The man walked away and said, 'Good day'
And went down by the stream.
The boy needed a chairman,
So he asked all of his mates,
Some said no, some said yeah,
One boy said he doesn't really care.
They all watched in fear, who's he going to pick?
Then suddenly he shouted a boy named Nick!

Chloe New (12)
The Sholing Technology College, Southampton

I Give You A . . .

I give you a heart full of love
It's got wings so it can fly like a dove
It flies swiftly through Heaven like an angel
It smells of fresh flowers and strawberries
Love is understanding and never lets you down

I give you an arrow dipped in chocolate
Love is like an angel
And connects you to the person you adore
When you hold it, it is so soft
That you could fall asleep holding it.

Stephanie Anders (13)
The Sholing Technology College, Southampton

My Pet Cat!

He's always outside catching the bees
When he comes back, he smells like trees
And tries to get dinner from whoever he sees
He is so lazy, always asleep
I look in his eyes and know he's to keep
And as I am sat, I think of my cat
Eight dinner Alfie, laid on the mat!

Sofia Hadzidimitriou (12)
The Sholing Technology College, Southampton

A Star Poem

Shining bright in the night sky
It guides my way as I pass by
It is there all night twinkling
As if it is singing
Across the night sky
They are sprinkled
As I passed by they twinkled.

Gemma Croxall (12)
The Sholing Technology College, Southampton

Special Friends

If you were a flower
I would pick you
If you were a dog
I would walk you
No matter what you say
I would be your friend all day, every day
Friends are so special
Never let them down
Because if you let them down
They won't stay around.

Emily Veal (12)
The Sholing Technology College, Southampton

Act Of Terror

It was a normal day. Petty
squabbles, small excitements, little
fears. So when we got the news, we
didn't believe it.
We were wrong.
It was a nightmare. You felt
detached; it was
unreal.
Shocked, shaken, afraid,
some in tears, the rest
clustering around trying helplessly
to give comfort. Desperately
trying to make contact. Whispered
words to calm fears.
The news filters through - the news we barely dared
to hope for. Those who have heard are rejoicing; others
wait in silent, lonely uncertainty.
Chaos. Lessons disrupted. Too
horrified
to work. Wasn't this
what they wanted? If we
are too frightened to move, then haven't
they won? Those
who were claimed, is this what they would want?
No. We must live on, live
on. It seems
disloyal. We must carry on, not forget but
Carry on.

Naomi Fish (13)
Tolworth Girls' School, Surbiton

Sour Grapes

The grapes have long turned sour,
The bread is spotted with mould.
She sits in all her splendour,
The young bride since turned old.
Her roses have wilted, sad memories,
Her veil has turned yellow with age,
She's still got her prayer book open,
But never did she turn a page.
The food is still untouched,
The wedding cake crawling with flies,
She never took a bite.
Her love was made of lies.
The confetti, discarded, unopened,
The garish hues paled,
It didn't bring much luck,
Her marriage still failed.
On that wedding morning,
When she held the knife
And the droplets of blood flowed
As she took her life.
Now she doesn't move,
Still lying there in respect,
Gone is this girl,
Whose life was perfect.

Judith Zendle (14)
Tolworth Girls' School, Surbiton

Commitments

We made commitments for a reason,
They were meant to keep us together,
Together through the seasons,
Seasons that last forever.

Karen Wood (14)
Tolworth Girls' School, Surbiton

Betrayal

The moment I saw you
My heart skipped a beat.
My head all light and I could feel the heat.
You were seeing someone else
And to have me you broke her heart.
Why couldn't I see you would do the same to me?
Happiness and joy, I loved you so much
And they weren't just words they came from the heart.
I was so scared and foolish so I had to end it.
Your face so sad, I cannot forget it.
I still love you, though I pretend I don't.
You and I have had other crushes,
But you're the one who fills my heart and makes me blush,
We went without speaking but suddenly you said hi.
Then told me you can't and that you're in love with me, so bye.
I couldn't put up with all your lies and betrayal.
So I told you that I had moved on.
How could you, the person I loved, cause me so much hate?
Oh well, now it's too late.
But the fact still stands I hate the fact
I don't hate you at all, because I'm
Deeply in love with you still.

Jade Phillips (14)
Tolworth Girls' School, Surbiton

Rose!

Rose was a beautiful flower,
Who had a secret power,
She made the grass green,
So kind and not mean,
But to pets her taste was so sour.

Fagae Asghari (14)
Tolworth Girls' School, Surbiton

Why Me?

I wish I wasn't the one who cried
The one who slept with her mum at night
Why is it always me alone?
But I never even dare to let out a moan
Why am I always last to be picked
Or worse yet, be forgotten again?
Why me? . . . Did I really deserve this?

I wanted to be popular
I did . . . I did . . .
But no one ever chose to be friends with me
I was just the girl in her baggy trousers
And over-large T-shirts
The girl no one noticed

All I ever wanted was to be liked
Have a bit of fun and respect
But now it's too late
I had to do it . . .
I had to end my pain!

Hannah Kerly (14)
Tolworth Girls' School, Surbiton

The Storm

The storm is a roaring lion,
Fiery and violent,
Chasing after his prey,
As he jumps and ravishes the bleating deer,
The lion gulps it down,
Letting out a bellowing roar,
Rolling rapidly along the sandy bank,
He dives into the river,
To find the next unwilling victim,
For his extravagant dinner.

Alice Green (14)
Tolworth Girls' School, Surbiton

Lifeless

Lifeless!

Yesterday, I can't believe,
He left me.

What did I do wrong?
I'm so upset!
Aren't weddings meant to be one of the happiest
Days of your life?
So why wasn't mine?
When we take our vows
Aren't you meant to be faithful?
I was left standing alone, just waiting.
Waiting for him to turn up, he never did!
Where is he?
I'm alone here!
All my effort has been ruined and wasted,
The thought of you drives me crazy.

I'm here sitting in my dress,
Not moved!
The food is all still laid out,
The flowers are starting to wilt,
Hope I've left you full of guilt.

Time has stopped.

Katie Launder Glass (14)
Tolworth Girls' School, Surbiton

Lamentations Of An Old Man

The house is an old man,
With thin long limbs,
A cracked long face,
And an abundance of old belongings.
The brown old sofa that he sat on
And the bare wood, his walking cane,
The creaking stairs, old tired feet,
Calloused and bridged.
The roof, a hat worn so many times fishing,
The holes let fish water through,
The glasses cracked and unnoticed,
Like windows into the soul.
The soul, empty, magnolia coloured.
The wallpaper, wrinkled skin, peeling
Off the once healthy body,
A brown door, a bourbon biscuit,
Half-eaten by worms.
Old 'house' man creaks and groans as the wind blows,
Smells of talcum powder and sweat,
Disused and decaying away.
At 7 asleep the lights off inside,
An air raid shelter in the garden,
A memory of the past,
The old man with not much left to live for,
Smiles as a new day is born.

Robyn Ward (14)
Tolworth Girls' School, Surbiton

Forever Not . . .

At first your love was passionate and true,
You swept me off my feet, the world was ours.
Together forever, you made me feel new,
You bought me presents, chocolates and flowers.
But soon our love died; it seemed to change,
We thought we could get through these awful days.
Hours passed by, we had to rearrange,
The magic passed by, was it a phase?
We drifted apart, for that I am sad,
For now I am crying, I want you back.
Of all the things it really made me mad,
I wonder what it was, that I did lack?
Onwards and upwards, I'll get over you,
Our love has ended, what will you do?

Alka Patel (14)
Tolworth Girls' School, Surbiton

An Unloved Secret

It stood there proud and tall, a unicorn
Was being shadows by a new found queen.
A well kept secret was soon to be born,
Kept in a tower waiting to be seen.
Her freedom is her only desire,
Idolised by children as their new princess.
A prisoner surrounded by fire,
Gifts will be given, a beautiful dress.
Time will pass and still she will be hidden.
Unknown to her the strength of her magic,
Rushed away to the site that's forbidden,
Isolated, her future is tragic.
Unloved by her mother, it hurts inside,
This is my life, yet I still have my pride.

Gurpreet Kalsi (14)
Tolworth Girls' School, Surbiton

Forgotten

July 1, all is quiet in the trench,
The chums waiting to attack.
Birdsong. England. A cup of tea.
A foreign dream.

The whistle sounds, shattered.
Tea forgotten, I go over the top,
Thank God for that extra ration of rum . . .
Dutch courage. I follow orders into

The mouth of Hell. No-man's-land.
Mud. water, gunshot, shell fire.
The noise torments my brain.
Gunshot, in my chest, I feel only

Pain. Falling down. I half drown.
Turning, I see the sky. Do we deserve to die?
I now see that this war was a lie.
I think of my loved ones, and I'm gone. Forgotten.

She walks through the rows of stones,
The graves of men lost in the war.
She looks on and does not feel alone,
As the soldiers, gone to rest, stand as before.

Sophie Finney (15)
Tormead School, Guildford

Epitaph 1916

'Known unto God'
They write on his grave
But as they write this they lie,
As he does, beneath the ground.

For he is known to his mother,
His father, his brother,
His pals, the men he lies beside,
To me.

He is known in the hearts
Of those that loved him,
In the whispers of laughter,
The echoes of sunshine that remain.

I weep for him,
With tears of pride.
I wear my grief on my sleeve
And my heart swells.

I know not which stone to visit,
No flowers I lay by,
But when I hear his name and remember,
I smile as I cry.

Emily Adams-Cairns (15)
Tormead School, Guildford

Questioned Authority

Don't look at me like that,
With scorn embedded in your furrowed brow,
Dull emptiness reflecting in your eyes.
Don't speak to me like that, for now,
I understand that all is left are lies.

Tilt down your nose from high up in the air
And take a look around your sergeant's boots.
Inspect the slime and bones of men who died,
Notice that poor boy who shuts his eyes - then shoots.
Who said that peace and war come side by side?

Don't point your gun at me,
We are both men and in our veins, men's blood.
My fate is not decided by the moon,
But by that weapon plastered in God's mud.
We are a damaged mass of soldier toys,
A thousand legs of tin in children's hands.
We once were civil men, now foolish boys,
With turmoil in our heads which no one understands.

Claire Hallybone (15)
Tormead School, Guildford

Summer

Swimming in the pool
Trying to get cool
Having a lot of fun
In the scorching sun
We will play with the ball
Until the rain will fall

Summer is over, it is bad
We can't help feeling sad.

Paige Harper (10)
Trevelyan Middle School, Windsor

War

It's always broadcast on TV,
Reported in the newspapers and the magazines,
A topic that we can't escape,
A topic that everyone surely must hate,
Heartbroken faces, crushed expressions,
People's lives filled with aggressions,
Something we could all surely live without,
Something that makes me want to shout,
It ruins tonnes of people's lives,
Its bombs, its grenades, its guns, its knives,
Innocent people get unnecessarily killed,
Their families are lost, their blood is spilled,
Surely this doesn't have to be?
It wouldn't if it were up to me.

Kirstie Harman (11)
Trevelyan Middle School, Windsor

Summer - Haikus

In the summertime
I like to swim in the sea
I like to have fun

When the sea is hot
The sea is so beautiful
Beautiful and smooth.

Jack Harrold (10)
Trevelyan Middle School, Windsor

Snow

Drifting down in layers,
Creating a vast blanket of white,
Hiding houses,
Covering cars,
Tinting trees.

James Napier (10)
Trevelyan Middle School, Windsor

The Gigantic Volcano

The gigantic volcano,
That erupts every century.
Terrifying, enormous, bubbly,
It's like a huge mountain,
With blood running down.
Like a still hill
And all of a sudden
A load of fire comes
Out the top.
It makes me feel
Horrified,
Like a plain
Person that never
Wants to be seen
Or heard from again.
The gigantic volcano,
That reminds us of the
Deaths of loads of people.

Tessa Kirby (10)
Trevelyan Middle School, Windsor

A Greek Temple

A Greek temple
A gateway to the gods
Old and great and ruined
Like a palace
Like gold
A respected place
Like I built its respect
A Greek temple
Reminds me the skilled built many.

Thomas Moran (10)
Trevelyan Middle School, Windsor

What Is The Point Of A Fish?

(Inspired by 'What Is The Point Of A Goldifish?' by Stewart Henderson)

What is the point of a fish?
All they do is swim in a dish.
You can't take them for a walk,
You can't make them chat and talk.
What is the point of a fish?

What is the point of a fish?
They swim in a beautiful dish.
They are colourful and bright,
They glow in the night,
That is the point of a fish!

Angela Cracknell (10)
Trevelyan Middle School, Windsor

Gold

Gold
Everyone likes it
Round, shiny, valuable
Like the yellow sun
As wanted as the winning lottery ticket
It makes me feel rich
Like a god
But reminds me the lengths people will go to.

Bryce Kane (11)
Trevelyan Middle School, Windsor

My Dog

My dog is a small, fluffy little thing,
He trundles around waiting to be found

And when I do, he runs away,
I swim in the pool, he comes in too.

He sometimes dances to his favourite tunes.

Lottie Mudge (10)
Trevelyan Middle School, Windsor

The Graceful Aeroplane

The graceful aeroplane
A modern way to travel
Huge, sleek, high-tech
Like a bird soaring through the sky
As long as a city
It makes me feel as though I'm higher than everyone
It makes me feel like I'm in a cloudy heaven
The graceful aeroplane
Reminds us how beautiful the atmosphere is.

Tom Flower (10)
Trevelyan Middle School, Windsor

The Storm

The storm
Creates huge waves
Raging, crashing, frothing
Is as fierce as a raging bull
Is as enormous as a giant
Makes me feel strong
Strong as a lion
The storm
Reminds us that everyone can be strong.

Robert Moran (11)
Trevelyan Middle School, Windsor

Lemony Snicket

Lemony Snicket's books are fun,
I enjoy the scenes where they run,
They are so cool,
His books really rule,
I read them out in the sun.

George Peryer (11)
Trevelyan Middle School, Windsor

Robin Hood

Robin Hood
Was an outlawed earl,
He took to the wood
With a lovely girl
And there and then,
There was lord and queen
Of a band of men,
In Lincoln green -
There was Scarlet Will
And Allan a Dale
And great big Little John-o
And Friar Tuck, that fat old buck
And Much the Miller's son-o!

Andrew Holmes (10)
Trevelyan Middle School, Windsor

The Great Statue Of Liberty

The great Statue of Liberty
It was built in France in 1884
It's gigantic, enormous, big
And it is like a giant person
Pointing to the sky
Like a 300ft giant
When I look at it, it feels
Like it will fall on me
It makes me feel really small
The great Statue of Liberty
Makes me think of how small
I am and how big the Statue of Liberty is.

Grant White (10)
Trevelyan Middle School, Windsor

My Kitten Kennings

Strong teeth
Sharp claws
Cheeky kitten
Little mitten
Looks cute
No mute
Big pouncer
No stronger
Sly walker
Loud talker
Fluffy fur
Cute purr.

Mellissa Watson (11)
Trevelyan Middle School, Windsor

The Red Rose

The red rose
Grown just ten days ago
Tall, spiky and strong
Spiky like barbed wire
Touch it and bleed like anything
It makes me feel quite small
I feel like a cat
The same size as the rose
It reminds me how long
I live.

Emily Gifford (10)
Trevelyan Middle School, Windsor

The Sphinx

The sphinx
It's half tiger, half man
Enormous, strong, ancient
Like a tiger with its prey
Like a god in the heavens
It makes me feel excited
Like a bird twittering
The sphinx
Reminds me how dangerous
Tigers are.

Blair McHarg (10)
Trevelyan Middle School, Windsor

Tree

The tall great tree
Non-stop growing
Tall, striking, miserable
Like a lonely woman living on her own
Ruling the woods
It makes me feel small
Like a feather floating
The tall great tree
Reminding us we will never be as great.

Gabby Killick (11)
Trevelyan Middle School, Windsor

Sport

S is for swimming, 'Go Katie, go!'
P is for pole-vaulting, how high can you jump?
O is for Olympics, will we win the 2012 bid?
R is for running, look at Kelly go.
T is for tennis, 'Go on Henman!'
S is for sports that I love.

Hannah Ward (11)
Trevelyan Middle School, Windsor

The Amazing Tiger

The amazing tiger
Beautifully coloured
Strong, fierce, safe
Like the chief of the jungle
As strong as he can be
It makes me feel like roaring
Like one of my best friends
The amazing tiger
Tells us how much we should keep animals safe.

Grace Bradbury (10)
Trevelyan Middle School, Windsor

The Beautiful Flower

The beautiful flower
It is the only one in the world
Pretty, colourful, big
As beautiful as a princess
As yellow as a sun
It makes me feel happy
Like it's Christmas
The beautiful flower
It makes me think how nice nature can be.

Amy Balchin (10)
Trevelyan Middle School, Windsor

Winter

W ind blowing, the leaves gushing around
 I n the house snuggled up, cosy watching TV, how warm are we!
N ovember is so icy cold when the wind blows a strong gale
T ormenting weather spoiling our playtime
E very night Christmas gets closer and the excitement sets in
R ain falling *pitter patter* to the ground, oh how wet we are!

Sophie Ellis (11)
Trevelyan Middle School, Windsor

The Great Ocean

The great ocean,
Where boats have come and gone.
Deep, blue, wavy,
Like a huge wall towering over the beach.
Like horses galloping down the seabed.
I feel so young when I think of it,
Like a newborn baby.
The great ocean,
Reminds us how small we are.

Ria Chaudry (10)
Trevelyan Middle School, Windsor

A Wide Ocean

A wide ocean created by water
Huge, salty, murky
Like a huge blue cloth
Like a bird flapping its wings
It makes me feel small
Like a tiny fish swimming at the bottom of the big ocean
A wide ocean
Reminds us of how huge the sea is.

Rosie Wege (10)
Trevelyan Middle School, Windsor

A Diamond

Extremely rare
It's small, shiny, divine
Like a glittering star
It's like a pure drop of water
It makes me feel ugly
Like a rock
A diamond
It reminds me of how elegant things are.

Lewis Ouaret (10)
Trevelyan Middle School, Windsor

The High Cloud

The high cloud
In the blue sky
High, white, huge
Like a ball of cotton wool
Like a white woolly hat
I feel small
I feel like a tiny ant
The high cloud
It reminds us how high it could be.

Shanice Smith (10)
Trevelyan Middle School, Windsor

Windsor Castle

Windsor Castle
Built years ago
Old, great and rusty
It's like a solid warrior standing tall
It's like a fort in the east
It makes me feel so weak
Like a person everybody could beat up
Windsor Castle
Reminds us how strong we are.

Henry Kidman (10)
Trevelyan Middle School, Windsor

The Night Sky

The moon shone high in the sky,
Its reflection glistening onto the lake,
The stars twinkled like diamonds,
How beautiful it is
And how everyone says the moon keeps
Them awake at night.

Ben Chubb (10)
Trevelyan Middle School, Windsor

Snow

The lovely white stuff that falls down
On us at wintertime.
Children love to play in it
But most grown-ups stay inside.

Something nice to play in,
We call it snow.
Santa's also part of it,
Ho, ho, ho.

Zoe Cunningham (10)
Trevelyan Middle School, Windsor

The Flying Scotsman

The Flying Scotsman
King's Cross to Edinburgh
Puffing, speeding, towering
Like a giant strolling past
Like a dragon breathing smoke
It makes me feel small
Like I'm just a little nothing
The Flying Scotsman
It is a legend.

Nick Boyd (10)
Trevelyan Middle School, Windsor

A Waterfall

A waterfall
Made from rocks and formed by hills
Huge, tall, endless
Like a volcano erupting with water
Like the sea rolling in from the horizon
It makes me feel tiny
A waterfall
Reminds us of running water.

Esther Rowell (10)
Trevelyan Middle School, Windsor

Shopping!

When I go shopping,
I have to cross a zebra crossing,
I like to buy bags,
Other people buy flags.
There's lots of things in the shop,
Sometimes you have so much, you might drop.
You can buy all sorts of stuff,
You can even get clothes with fluff
And that's what happens when you go
Shopping!

Holly Foulkes (10)
Trevelyan Middle School, Windsor

Computers

C omputers are cool!
O h, you've got to check them out.
M y computer is great.
P eople that have them are cool.
U can do lots of stuff on them.
T ell others.
E veryone will like them.
R eally cool.
S o fun.

Nawaz Mahmood (10)
Trevelyan Middle School, Windsor

The Old Man

There was an old man
Who liked to swim
And he was incredibly dim
He got in the pool
And looked like a fool
So everyone laughed at him!

Ian Porter (11)
Trevelyan Middle School, Windsor

Sorry

Sorry is sometimes hard to say when you've spoken your mind.
It wasn't right, seems oh so wrong,
It was mean of me to say that,
But I didn't mean that, so why did I just say it?

There are two kinds of sorry,
One that you say and one that you mean!
But do I want to say it . . . *no!*
The truth is everyone's sorry sometimes,
It just hurts to admit that you are.
Why can't I say it? . . . I do not know.
Hold on, here goes, 'I'm sorry!'
Now excuse me while I throw!

Harriet O'Donnell (11)
Trevelyan Middle School, Windsor

The Swinging Monkey

The swinging monkey
Swings from tree to tree
Small, skinny, fast
He is like a bird going from tree to tree
And eats like a pig
I feel like he is my best friend
I feel like I am a monkey like him
The swinging monkey
He makes me think
I wish they would stop chopping
All the trees down!

Jennifer Sylivestrou (10)
Trevelyan Middle School, Windsor

Junior Jail

I'm a bad boy in jail.
I wish I could get bail.
I sleep in a cell,
This feels like Hell.
I live with my crew,
We have cell loos.

I'm not in Heaven,
Some aren't eleven.
The food is glum,
Friends rarely come.
The beds are bleak,
The ceilings leak.
There are sometimes rats,
But no sign of cats.
So God help me,
I want to be free.

Ashley Britton (11)
Trevelyan Middle School, Windsor

The Puddle

The puddles
As deep as the ocean
Clear, big, wide
Like a big blob of ink
Like a wild ocean
It makes me feel thirsty
I feel like a big, thirsty bear
A puddle
It makes me think how
Thirsty humans can be.

Michael Irvine (10)
Trevelyan Middle School, Windsor

Drip Drop

Drip, drop, drip, drop,
Each has a burst of life,
Fresh from a tap, life begins,
So far we have no sins.

Drip, drop, drip, drop,
Falling through the drain,
Down the pipes, rushing silent,
Teenager, becoming violent.

Drip, drop, drip, drop,
Springs and streams,
A few years gone,
Something's always going on.

Drip, drop, drip, drop,
Getting older, getting pruned,
Engaged in love by the river,
But it's cold, we start to shiver.

Drip, drop, drip, drop,
We come towards the end,
We enter the water holders above,
The clouds of course, white as a dove.

Drip, drop, drip, drop,
God, the tap, has let us go,
But now we have to evaporate,
Through the clouds, into the gate.

Cherrie Clarke (13)
Wildern School, Southampton

When I'm With You

When I'm with you
My soul's set free
To be the true me
You see what no one else sees
When I'm with you

When you're around
My fears - they lift
My spirit uplifts
To another world I drift
When you're around

When you are close
A warmth I feel
My wounds are healed
My dreams are sealed
When you are close

When I'm with you
I love you.

Victoria Morley (13)
Wildern School, Southampton

Take A Second

Sometimes in the morning when I awake,
I stop, think and look at my mistakes,
But life's too short to dwell on the past,
Life moves forward, it's drifting fast.
So I get ready and get on with my day
And go about the same old way.
But are we all content or are some on the brink?
That's why it's nice to take a second and think.

Lucy French (14)
Windsor Girls' School, Windsor

Mum, I Know I've Done Wrong

Mum, I know I've done wrong and it was my entire fault
Can you please ground me till the end of the month?
I know I should say, 'O, Sis, I love you so much
And I should not have shoved your head in the rabbit hutch.'

I know I'm the oldest and should set examples
And not have been selfish and eaten the apple crumble.
As the day goes by, my love for you will never die
And it was not true that I wanted to shoot you in-between the eyes.

When my homies come round,
Feel free to hang around,
They think you're gangster and totally cool
And do not want to drown you in the local swimming pool.

Hey Sis, you're the best and I love you so much,
Your sweetness is adorable giving you the finishing touch.
Mum, I know I've done wrong and it was my entire fault,
Can you please ground me till the end of the month?

Terrie Clements (14)
Windsor Girls' School, Windsor

A Sonnet

Shall I compare thee to a teddy bear?
You hug me when I need it, not want it
And cuddle me when I've had a nightmare.
You annoy me sometimes, well, just a bit,
But you love me too much for me to mind
And I can quickly forgive and forget.
The thread that you and I together bind,
Tightens each day from our love and respect,
The strength of rope it so easily builds,
You guide my way in this vast open land,
Hide me from the pain and the hurt, you shield,
Our love can form a never-ending band,
So will you love me always, and me - you?
As you show me my way, I'll show yours too.

Alice Wigley (14)
Windsor Girls' School, Windsor

Give Us Some More

Why don't you give us some more homework?
We really don't have enough.
Just a few more essays, they really aren't that tough,
Just a few more, we don't have anything else to do,
Come to think of it, why not give us an extra report or two?
Our social lives no longer matter to us any more,
We want more homework, we don't find it a bore,
Hour after hour, day after day,
We don't mind slaving away,
We'll make sure it's on time, we'll make sure it's neat and good,
Then we'll do some revision, cos we know that we should,
We can't wait till our exams, we love them a lot,
Revision 24 hours a day, so our brains don't rot,
We get so much homework, we'll be doing it till we're dead,
Stuff all our social lives; let's do homework instead!

Sally Wege (14)
Windsor Girls' School, Windsor

Our World

The world is a humungous place,
A massive circle with only one face.

Hundreds of countries with all different races,
Many of them live in some troublesome places.

Poverty, hunger, natural disasters,
Those with money the ultimate masters.

Fighting, killing for much more wealth,
Poor people concerned only with health.

Innocent people dying each day,
While the evil and greedy are free to play.

The world is suffering from man's carelessness,
In the end it will finish in one terrible mess.

Mica Lisk (14)
Windsor Girls' School, Windsor

My Suicide

You tempt me with your sharp good looks
Your razor-sharp edges lure me in
There you are just lying there
You are my biggest sin

No one's trying to stop me do this
No one even cares about me
This feels so right to gain pain
Why can't anyone wake up and see?

I need your help with this
Help me with my problem, please
Why do you just sit and stare?
Why do you just tease?

I need someone to look after me
I need someone to stay
I need someone to say to me
'Everything will be OK'

If anyone really cared
They'd help me through my suicide
Instead they all just sit there
Looking, while I died inside.

Grace Prior (14)
Windsor Girls' School, Windsor

Exam Recipe

Take any number of useless facts,
Find a class of empty brains
And start cramming the info in.

Watch them learn, remember and forget,
All flustered and panicked,
Even the teacher's pet.

Add in revision guides and homework,
Stir well, till their brains begin to fizzle
And everything you told them is *gone*.

Move mixture to the exam room,
Separate and seat in alphabetical order,
Where the dreaded test does loom.

Silence except the humming of working,
Then you add the heat with only five minutes left,
Finally, the end and your mixture is hot and glazed over.

Leave to cool for at least half an hour,
The mood rises and brightens,
No longer sour.

Kate Parsonage (14)
Windsor Girls' School, Windsor

Poet's Block

Writing a poem
Is a waste of time,
Spending hours
Getting words to rhyme.

As I think harder
My brain goes dead,
My imagination
Must be fed.

My teacher tells me
To think a bit more.
'Hurry up, Louise
You did much better before!'

I can't write a poem
It's driving me mad
And when the bell rings
I am extremely glad.

I need to escape,
I need to get out,
But I stop dead
As the teacher shouts

'Bring your brains next lesson,
We are continuing poetry.'
The whole class cheer
But the teacher looks at me.

I gasp at the thought
Writing a poem is supposed to be fun,
But it's just so hard,
I don't think I'll *ever* write one!

Louise Whitehouse (14)
Windsor Girls' School, Windsor

Just Got To Start

Discriminated for what you believe
And what you like,
It has to stop,
We'll go on strike!
No chance to grow,
You'll never know,
What life could be
And what there is for us to see.
When life starts for you,
Don't be afraid,
You have your talents,
You've got it made.
Follow your dreams,
Listen to your heart,
Here's a new journey,
You've just got to start!

Justine Chambers (14)
Windsor Girls' School, Windsor

What Earth Means To Me

Earth brings happiness
Earth brings sadness
Earth brings birth
Earth brings death
Earth is paradise
Earth is Hell
Earth is relaxing
Earth is evil
Earth brings life . . .
Life is random!

Amy Hiskett (14)
Windsor Girls' School, Windsor

Dad

I love the way you talk to me
I love the way you care
I love the way you never call
When you're not always there

I love the way you buy me treats
And always take me out
I love the way you used smack
Especially when you shout

I love the way your hand goes high
The way you used to clout
I love the way since I was small
You've never been about

I love it when we used to laugh
And even more when I cry
But now you're gone
I'm all alone
It's me, myself and I.

Chantelle McPadden (14)
Windsor Girls' School, Windsor

Brain

What's the point of a brain?
It just drives me insane
It wastes space in my head
And it's heavy like lead

It never works when it's told
Just sits there freezing cold
It can't hold one small fact
Let alone one whole act

It eats quick as a flash
But for work it's mish mash
I'm sure it's stuffed full of fluff
And everything else in life is tough

So what is the point of it
It's meant to do its bit
But my brain refuses
And does as it chooses.

Astrid Crawley (14)
Windsor Girls' School, Windsor

Five Portions A Day

Yes, Mum,
Of course I should eat that,
That little segment of orange,
Which will keep me healthy
For the rest of my happy life.
As soon as I eat that,
I'll be jumping around,
Leaping about,
As fit as a fiddle.
In fact, eat too much fruit
And I'll have to eat more junk food,
To counteract my healthiness,
Too many vegetables
And I'll go down in world records
'Healthiest person ever!'
So, yes Mum,
Of course I'll eat that,
I'll do whatever you say.

Maisie Johnson (13)
Windsor Girls' School, Windsor